THE WHEELS ON THE BUS

My Journey as a School Bus Driver

BRENDA LEE MERKLEY

The Wheels on the Bus
Copyright © 2021 by Brenda Lee Merkley

All rights reserved. No part of this publication may be reproduced, distributed, or transmitted in any form or by any means, including photocopying, recording, or other electronic or mechanical methods, without the prior written permission of the author, except in the case of brief quotations embodied in critical reviews and certain other non-commercial uses permitted by copyright law.

Scripture taken from the Holy Bible, NEW INTERNATIONAL VERSION®, NIV® Copyright © 1973, 1978, 1984, 2011 by Biblica, Inc.® Used by permission. All rights reserved worldwide.

tellwell

Tellwell Talent
www.tellwell.ca

ISBN
978-0-2288-5518-7 (Paperback)
978-0-2288-5519-4 (eBook)

This book is for any school bus driver who has ever counted down the days to: the Christmas break, Spring Break, Easter break, and finally the Summer break.

And to every student who rode route #22 to Heritage Heights (circa 2013 ongoing)

TABLE OF CONTENTS

Foreword vii

Chapter 1	The Picker and the Tattler 1
Chapter 2	Frequently Asked Questions 6
Chapter 3	Driving Miss Emma! 11
Chapter 4	Faith on the Bus 20
Chapter 5	Our Little Busing Company 25
Chapter 6	Are You Having Fun Yet? 31
Chapter 7	From the Mouth of Babes 38
Chapter 8	Odds and Sods 42
Chapter 9	U-Turns 47
Chapter 10	How Did I Get Here? 59
Chapter 11	And So the Journey Starts 70
Chapter 12	Finding Jesus in Bluefields, Nicaragua (Not That He Was Lost) 76
Chapter 13	Schooling Should Not Be a Privilege ... 87
Chapter 14	Seeing Is Believing 98
Chapter 15	Back Home 103
Chapter 16	COVID-19 109
Chapter 17	Back on the bus…year 8 116

Acknowledgements 123

FOREWORD

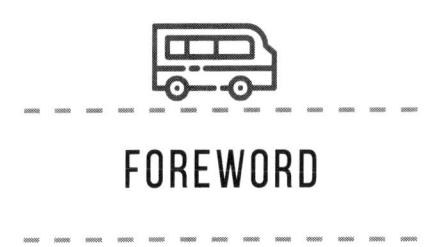

"An invisible thread connects those who are destined to meet, regardless of time, place, and circumstance. The thread may stretch or tangle. But it will never break."

—Ancient Chinese Proverb

I've always felt there was a book in me somewhere (which might explain the indigestion). I just didn't know what it would be about. I used to write and dabble with poetry when I was younger, and rhymes and puns have always interested me. I love reading today; it's probably one of my favourite pastimes. I have a hoard of books in my cupboard that I'm always adding to, and my varied interests range from historical dramas to thrillers. I love a good plot, a whodunit. My high school English Lit teacher, Mr. Brunet, had a profound impact on me. He taught Shakespeare, and I loved it. He also said something that is still with me today: If when you read a book, you lose yourself in the character and actually become the character—if you eat, live, and breathe the character— that is the sign that the book was written by a good author. I still reflect on those words when I come across a book I just can't put down.

This book came about because I shared a few of my bus stories with a friend. She thought they were funny and encouraged me to put them on paper. So I started. As I wrote, I realized that I wanted to explain to the reader how I came to be a bus driver. I didn't just wake up one morning and think, *Gee, I want to be a bus driver!* NOT! Are you kidding me?

Everyone has a journey to travel. I believe wholeheartedly that my path was mapped out from the beginning of my existence. God knew, and still knows, exactly what my course will be. Some of the roads I've travelled have been uphill, downhill, slippery, straight, curved, dead ends, and never ending. Yet I'm right where I'm supposed to be. It may have taken a little longer to get here due to my total lack of directional skills, but here I am!

God has gifted me with a sense of humour. This has proven to be a blessing at times (like when dealing with a 250-pound biker) and also a curse (like when dealing with a 250-pound biker). But that's a story for another day. My story will take you in and around, and hopefully you can follow me.

I lived in Whitecourt, Alberta between 1994 and 1999. There I met an older gentleman, Joe, who had been a school bus driver for thirty years. He just raved and went on about how much he loved it. A bus driving position was available at that time, so I asked Joe what he thought about me training for it. I was out of work at the time, and I thought it would be an easy gig. Joe looked me right in the eye and asked, "Do you like children?"

NO! I don't. What does that have to do with anything? Joe suggested very strongly that I choose a different profession. I'm grateful I listened to him back then. Had I decided to go through with that plan, I'm sure I wouldn't have lasted at it. It wasn't the right time for me. But here I am twenty years later and 8sleeps away from the summer break, wrapping up 8 wonderful years as a school b us driver. I absolutely love my job!

CHAPTER ONE

THE PICKER AND THE TATTLER

"Brendaaaa! Charlie's picking his nose again!"

Ughhhh! These are words you really don't want to hear on the bus. Why is it that boys feel the need to pick their nose and then show it to girls? It's like they've just found a treasure and can't wait for everybody to see it, especially if that everybody is a girl in their classroom whom they're trying to impress. Why do girls need to tattle on the picker? And by tattling, I mean yelling it out so that three buses around us now know that Charlie is picking his nose.

Charlie, whom I will refer to as the picker, is in grade one. I love the little guy. When Charlie started taking the bus two years ago, he was only on it sporadically. His parents would drive him to school in the morning and then come to the school in the afternoon to bring him to my bus. Once he was on the bus, his mom or dad would drive home and meet him at the bus stop. This went on for quite a while. Dad was having a harder time letting go of his young boy.

Charlie loves being on the bus! He sits right up front, where I like to sit the youngest students to keep an eye on them. This was a new experience for Charlie and one that he quite enjoyed. He actually gets upset if Dad picks him up from the school to go to an appointment. Dad told me that he thought Charlie liked me better than him. Dad no longer comes to the school to make sure Charlie gets on the bus. He trusts that the boy will get home safely. He does still pick him up at the other end. This year, he's even allowing them to walk by themselves toward home while he stands at the corner and waits for him. *Sniff!* He's come such a long way in letting go of Charlie. Way to grow, Dad.

Kaliyah, who will be known as the tattler, is in grade one with Charlie. She started taking the bus when she entered kindergarten. She is Filipino and the most beautiful child I've ever seen, besides my own girl, with her chubby chipmunk cheeks and big, beautiful brown eyes that sparkle when she smiles her incredible smile. It looks like she has a wonderful secret to share with you. She just lights up from the inside, and I can't help but smile when I see her. All of her emotions, thoughts, and feelings are written on her face. She is so open.

From day one on the bus, she has been comfortable. It's like she's been riding forever. Some students are nervous if they've never been on a bus. They don't know what to expect, or what the dos and don'ts are. It's a whole new learning experience for them and can be a very anxious time. My job is to make the time I have with them as smooth and enjoyable as possible. Well, miss Kaliyah has no qualms about riding the bus. From the get-go, she let me and everybody else on the bus know she was here! What a chatterbox! Nonstop from the time I pick her up to when I deposit her at the school—a total of about twenty minutes. Some days I swear it's sixty minutes. For the most part, she's a total delight.

When the bell rings at 3:15 p.m. for dismissal, the students clamber onto the bus. I do a roll call in the afternoon and mark their attendance on my checklist. We have to wait for six minutes before we can leave at 3:21p.m. During that time, I make sure the students are sitting in their designated seats and that no backpacks, or anything else, are in the aisles. This is for safety reasons. My kids are great about this. We do emergency drills to keep on top of it. During this waiting time, I also walk up and down the aisle and chat with the kids to find out what's going on, how they're doing, or how the basketball tournament went on the weekend. Did you have a nice birthday yesterday? How was the field trip today? I just like making contact with them to let them know I'm here. This helps to cut down on mischief that might be brewing ... not that my kids would get up to no good. I have awesome students. But I enjoy chatting with them, and I think they like to be centred out and spoken to in a friendly manner. I joke with them and really try to LISTEN to them. I hear them. I find that's so important to little ones, and to the older students too. They get a kick out of me going to the back of the bus to check on them, and it's really neat to be allowed in their space for a few minutes.

One particular day, I was checking off my attendance list as the students were boarding. I had one eye on those entering the bus, and one eye and ear on those already in their seats. I have a big rear-view mirror that I look into and can see clear to the back of the bus. The kids know that I check quite often to see what they're doing. As I said, they're a great bunch, so I don't usually have any problem. But on this day, Kaliyah, who sits two seats behind me and directly across the aisle from Charlie, drew everyone's attention to poor Charlie by yelling out," OH GROSS! Charlie is picking his nose!" She then proceeded to explain the facts of life to the picker, and what is and isn't acceptable in society. This from a six-year-old girl. Charlie wasn't very concerned about what she was flapping about. I very calmly grabbed a Kleenex from the box I keep up front and walked over to the said picker, who by the way was still looking for a treasure. I handed him the Kleenex, smiled and winked at him, and went back to my seat. Kaliyah visibly shivered when I looked over at her. She was totally grossed out. *So, I thought, that's that. Let's carry on like we're all normal.*

The following week, this episode was all forgotten. There were more pressing matters at hand. The afternoon bell rang, and the children started loading on the bus. I walked the aisle and checked that were all sitting properly. They were chatting about the pop quiz, so-and-so throwing up at recess, and so on. I stopped to say hi to Kaliyah and ask how her day was. She looked right at me and asked me very loudly for all to hear, "How come Charlie always picks his nose?" I looked at this angelic little girl, her little face all scrunched up in a frown. She was thoroughly disgusted with the picker who was sitting within touching distance, and she has captured the attention of most of the students in a six-seat radius. All eyes were on me to see how I would handle it. You have to be so, so careful when dealing with kids. This is one of many lessons I've learned as a bus driver of six 8 years. I have to select every action, word, and nuance so carefully. If I don't, feelings can get hurt, and the whole thing can backfire. We're dealing with children here. I'm the adult, so I'm supposed to be the voice of reason and authority. HA! What I said and did at that moment could affect the picker and the tattler for years to come ... or at least till I got them home.

I looked over at Charlie; I looked back at Kaliyah. I looked up and saw a dozen kids crowded around us to see what would happen. I gently reached over and cupped my hands on either side of Kaliyah's face, moved my face close to hers, and looked directly at her beautiful eyes. I said, "Kaliyah honey, has Charlie picked your nose?"

She looked absolutely mortified. "NO!" she replied.

I asked her if Alex had picked her nose, and again she replied "NO!" She kind of giggled this time. Keep in mind that everybody was watching. Still holding her little face in my hands, I asked her if I had picked her nose. She laughed this time and said "NO!"

I said to her, "Kaliyah, who is the only person allowed to pick your nose?"

She replied, "ME!"

I said, "That's right, sweetheart, you are the only person allowed to pick your nose. Is that right?"

She nodded her head and said, "Yeah, that's right, Brenda.

"So," I said, "Charlie should be allowed to pick his own nose, shouldn't he?"

By now she was giggling like crazy. "Yes," she said, "Charlie can pick his own nose."

I looked over to Charlie, who was smiling up at me, and I said, "Kaliyah, if Charlie ever picks your nose, you let me know, OK? We'll deal with that."

I walked to my seat and turned to face all the students and said, "OK, we have a new rule on our bus. From now on, you can only pick your own nose, and let your neighbour pick theirs in peace. Now let's go home." I am pleased to announce that I have not heard anything more on this matter.

CHAPTER TWO

FREQUENTLY ASKED QUESTIONS

Owen (grade one): Brenda, what's the hammer for?

Me: To use on the kids who ask too many questions.

Owen: Oh! Brenda, how many questions is too many questions?

Me: Come here and I'll show you.

Kieran (grade one): Brenda, how come we don't have seat belts?

Me: The kids who were on the bus before you stole them.

Danika (grade one): Brenda, how come we don't have seat belts, but you do?

Me: I bought my own.

Elliot (grade two): Brenda, how come we don't have seat belts?

Me: Your parents couldn't afford to buy them after paying for the school fees.

Connor (grade one): Brenda, how come we don't have seat belts?

Me: WHAT? We don't? You're kidding!

Chris (grade four): Brenda, what's the duct tape for?

Me: When I run out of room on the bus, I start taping students to the roof.

Chris, Elliot, Kieran, and Michael scream: Brenda, can you tape us to the roof of the bus?

Me: Don't tempt me, boys.

Ava (grade two): Brenda, what's the fire extinguisher for?

Me: I work as a part-time fire fighter. If I get a call, I'm ready to go.

Ava: Have you ever gotten a call?

Me: I don't know. I can't answer the phone when I'm driving the bus.

Ava: Well, if you did get a call, what would you do with us kids?

Me: Take you with me.

Ava: Oh! Cool!

Mariah (grade four): Brenda, how old are you?

Me: Fifty-five

Mariah: WHOA!

Me: What? It's not that old!

Mariah: OK.

Alex (grade three): Brenda, do you colour your hair?

Me: Yes

Alex: I thought so. My grandma colours hers too.

Sienna (grade two): Brenda, how long have you been driving a bus?

Me: Six years now.

Sienna: How old were you when you started driving a bus?

Me: Fifty-two

Sienna (counting in her precious little head): WOW!

Me: Rotten kid.

Ryker (grade one): Brenda, do you gots a Kleenex?

Me (trying to teach proper English): Do you gots a Kleenex?

Ryker: No, I don't. I'm asking if you got one.

Me: Aaargh! The proper way to ask for that is, "Brenda, do you have a Kleenex?" Try that.

Ryker (sigh): Brenda, do you HAVE a Kleenex?

Me: Well, yes, I do. Would you like a Kleenex?

Ryker: No, I don't need one, but my brother Ronin does. His nose is bleeding all over the bus seat.

Me: DOH! Rotten kids.

Last day of school

Massimo (grade one): Brenda, why are you crying?

Me: I'm just going to miss you guys so much!

Massimo: I've never seen anybody cry and smile at the same time before. Are you dancing?

First day of school

Massimo (grade two): Brenda, why are you crying again?

Me: I'm just so happy to see you all back!

Massimo: Brenda, it's OK. Please stop crying. Should I call someone? Why are all the bus drivers crying, Brenda?

I've come to realize over the course of 8 years that children just want to be heard. I know that so many of their queries and questions may seem silly or even unanswerable, but I've also come to realize that if I don't attempt to give them an answer of some kind, they'll keep asking the same question but in a different way. Once they have a satisfactory answer, they're on to the next big adventure. They just want to be acknowledged. To them, their question is very important. When they get their answer, they move on. When you poo- poo them, or just ignore them, I believe they feel like they and their ideas don't matter. By answering them, even if I tell them, "Gee, I don't know," I let them know that they're worth my time. I've seen time and time again that when I answer them as sincerely as I can, they appreciate it. It's pretty cool.

CHAPTER THREE

DRIVING MISS EMMA!

Emma started grade two the year I started driving. I can still picture her that first day. It was a beautiful September morning. All the children were decked out in their new school clothes, and their backpacks were laden with new pencils, crayons, and binders. Lunch kits were full of yummy snacks waiting to be eaten. You could feel the excitement of the first day! To be reunited with old friends, meet new ones, and anticipate who would be in their class and who would be their teacher. Most of them hadn't slept much the night before. It's just sooooo awesome and scary and fun and scary and new and scary. I felt exactly like they did. This was my first day. Oh my gosh! What was I thinking? Throughout my training, in-class and on the road, there were no kids in the picture. The bus was empty of these children. Now they were getting on the bus!

Emma glided onto the bus; I say glided because I really don't think her feet touched the ground. I saw this light emanating from her as I approached the bus stop. She was shining—all blonde curls with ribbons and bows, an incredible dress, and shiny new Mary Janes. She was first on.

I opened the door with a huge smile. She stood in front of me, stopped in her tracks, put her hands on her hips, and glared at me. "Who are you?" she asked.

She wasn't moving, so now the kids were waiting to come in. I said, "Hi, I'm Brenda. I'm your bus driver"

"No, you're not. Catherine is my bus driver." She actually tapped her foot! I told her that Catherine was now driving a different route and I'd now be driving this route. Again she said, "You're not Catherine." I told her to please have a seat, as we had to let the other students in. She sat in the first seat, staring straight ahead. She wasn't happy about this, no siree. As we drove toward school, I tried to make small talk, but she was having none of it. I was the enemy. I think I actually ducked a couple of times when I felt her glaring at me. Ouch! This was day one.

Over the next few weeks, we all settled into our routine on the bus. I was trying to learn all of the student's names, but they only had to learn mine. I had a big banner with my name on it by where I sat. Emma had a sister, Jordan, in grade four. Two opposite sides of the coin these two. Emma was frills and lace, every hair in place. She could have been a contender to be a true princess. Her sister, on the other hand, was jeans and T-shirts. Nothing really ruffled Jordan, except maybe when Emma was in her space. Typical siblings.

Emma eventually started talking to me. I'd ask her questions about her class; I knew she was also in dance after school. I chatted with her about her interests. She more often than not called me

Catherine. She'd had her as a bus driver for two years, so it was hard to break the habit of calling me anything else. Most days when she got on the bus, she would greet me with "Good morning, Catherine." I would say, "I'm Brenda. Good morning, Emma." She would grunt and shrug her shoulders and go to her seat. I was still not in her inner circle. If Catherine had decided to come back to my route, I would be just an afterthought.

One morning, Emma got on the bus and said, "Good morning, Catherine." I replied, "Good morning, Jordan." She stopped dead in the tracks, did a double take, spit out "I'm not Jordan!!!" I smiled at her and said "I'm not Catherine" Her mouth dropped, she looked deep at me, and smiled. She never called me Catherine again. This seemed to change the dynamics of our relationship from then on. She would get on the bus and start chatting with me, barely letting me get a word in. She'd still be chatting away as she was getting off the bus. I would wish her a good day and tell her to breathe. Some days, she was talking already as she was walking up the bus steps!

At this time, I had a new student start on the bus route. Her name was Skylar. She would be in the same class as Emma, so I sat them together on the bus. Skylar had been on the bus a couple of days when Emma had something to do after school so her mom picked her up. Skylar got on the bus and sat down. I explained that she would be sitting alone today. She was fine with that. She then asked me, "Brenda, what's that girl's name that I sit with?" I said her name was Emma and asked if she was OK sitting with her. She said, "Yeah, but she sure talks a lot."

I really, seriously tried not to laugh out loud. Out of the mouth of babes. I said, "Oh, you think so?" These two little girls were to become great friends.

I used to let the students eat on the bus; they would have a snack when they took their seats. They were usually pretty good about using the garbage can I kept up front. Do you know how much of a mess, Goldfish crackers can make when stepped on? I no longer allow eating on the bus, under the pretext of different allergies and also because of safety issues. If Johnny starts choking while I'm driving, he'll either be pounced on by four kids, or nobody will tell me. It's roughly ten minutes to get them home, so they're not going to starve. But early on when they could eat, Emma would eat her snack, usually dried seaweed.

One day when we were waiting for all the kids to load, Emma asked if I would like a piece of her snack. Having never tasted said snack, I said "Yes, please." She happily broke me off a little piece. I took it and put it in my mouth and promptly spit it out across the bus floor. "What is that? That's gross, Emma. How can you eat that?" I tried to spit the remainder of this noxious stuff off my tongue, along with the little piece glued to the roof of my mouth. I was trying not to gag! I looked over to Emma, who was howling. She thought it was hilarious. She was doubled over, she was laughing so hard. Rotten kid. I told her it was obviously an acquired taste.

Timing is of the utmost importance when you drive a school bus. I have a schedule and a time to get to every stop. If I'm delayed for any reason, it can set me back for every stop. This really doesn't seem like a big deal, but when I'm three or four minutes late to my next stop, and it's minus twenty outside while the kids are waiting on me, it is a big deal. If we drivers find ourselves in a situation where we're really behind, say ten or fifteen minutes, we radio dispatch, who then puts it on our website to let all parents know ASAP. It doesn't happen very often, but it can. It's great to have a backup plan in our corner. Word gets out there very quickly. To the best of my ability, I am at the same location every day at the same time.

One day, I arrived at Emma's stop and opened the door to let the students on. Emma stepped on the bus, stood in front of me while tapping her foot, and announced for all to hear, "Well, you're a little late this morning."

I glanced over to my clock and said, "Looks like I'm pretty close. I did have to wait at the last stop for a few seconds because Johnny was running for the bus. I'm not going to leave him behind." She harrumphed and walked off to her seat. I thought to myself, *why am I explaining myself to a seven-year- old?*

Well, as fate would have it, about a week later I pulled up to Emma's stop right on time and opened the door for the students. Far off down the street, I saw this blonde-headed little thing running to beat the band to catch the bus. Her arms were flailing, and she was yelling, "Wait for me! Wait for me!" Everybody on the bus, as if in stereo, yelled out "Emma's coming!" I very patiently waited for her, my stop signs out and my lights flashing, holding up traffic. She climbed onto the bus out of breath, panting, embarrassed, and sheepish. She quietly thanked me for waiting, and I smiled and winked at her and said, "Honey, I will never leave you behind." She never again remarked on my timeliness. She was such a gem.

My sister Debbie is eleven-and-a- half months older than me. For two weeks, we are the same age. That matters not one iota in the pecking order. She is the eldest; therefore, she is the boss of me. I can well understand the sibling rivalry that I see so often on the bus. I have numerous siblings on my route. I've had families of two, three, four, and even one family of five children for a year. There are constant battles, disagreements, tattling, and fighting going on. I've learned from experience to not get involved. Unless there is visible blood spurting out, or hair being pulled, I need to let them sort it out. Refereeing them in itself could be a full-time job.

Emma was not immune to the sister love/hate relationship. At times, she and Jordan were best friends, but at other times, not so much! If you picked on Emma, Jordan would protect her ... after all, she was the only one to pick on her. Typical sister stuff. Emma was so transparent; she wore every single emotion on her little cherub face. I could tell what kind of mood she was in as I pulled up to her stop. She was either smiling, scowling, crying, dancing, giggling, hissing, flapping her arms, or standing quietly (this last one did not happen very often). Many a time she would get on the bus complaining about how mean Jordan was to her. I would empathize with her, explaining how I also had an older sister who used to be mean to me too. But I also told her that we were very close now. I'd chat to her on the way to school, and by the time we'd arrive, her spirit would be lifted, and the incident all but forgotten.

Emma had been on my bus for about two years now. I was used to her different moods and ways. One day she got on the bus very quiet and withdrawn. I asked her if everything was OK, and she assured me all was good. She never said a word all the way to school. That afternoon when she got back on the bus, it was same thing. Solemn, sad looking, so little. I ventured again to ask if anything was bugging her, and again she said no. I had to believe her. I thought, *maybe she's just tired and had a late night. Maybe Jordan is bugging her.* This seemed unusual, as she usually forgot about whatever infraction had upset her by the afternoon bus ride. I let it go.

The next morning, Emma got on the bus, mumbled good morning, and went right to her seat. Normally she would chat with me about something really, really important. Again, I was a little concerned about this change in behaviour in my little chatterbox. When we arrived at the school, she walked off, head down and shoulders slumped, like she'd lost her best friend in the world. She wasn't even talking to her seat buddy, Skylar. Something was definitely wrong.

As Jordan exited the bus, I called to her to wait for a minute. I asked her if she knew if anything was wrong with Emma. I mentioned that I thought she looked awfully sad. Jordan said she hadn't noticed anything. So again, I had to let this go. I would wait and see. When you get to know these little people, you know when something is amiss. I had been around Emma enough to know that this was out of character.

That afternoon, I was anxious to get to the school. I was worried about her. I was so concerned that I actually talked to Catherine, her old bus driver, my predecessor. I asked her if Emma had displayed this kind of behaviour before. She said that if Jordan were bugging her she would get like this, but never for this long. Sure enough, Emma got on the bus in the afternoon looking so down and out. So dejected. My heart broke for her.

I dropped the students off and carried on to the bus compound. We as bus drivers have a list of all the students, their parents, phone numbers, and emergency contacts in a binder in our bus. This had to stop. I wasn't comfortable with the situation. I looked up Mom's number and dialled it. I've only had to call maybe three parents in the six years I've been driving. Nothing too serious, but just an issue to discuss with them. The parents I've dealt with are wonderful. They work with me and not against me. We all want what's best for their child.

Mom answered the phone, and I explained my concerns and worry over Emma. I told her that I didn't mean to step on any toes, but I was genuinely concerned. Mom thanked me profusely for bringing this to her attention. She would get on it right away. That was that. That's all I could do. I felt I had done the right thing by calling Mom. In our training as bus drivers, and in the numerous seminars and classes we take throughout the year in regard to school issues, I have learned and absorbed a few things. We are on the front line. Mine is the face your child will see first thing every day. I get to know your child—all their little personalities, their little quirks, their moods. I can tell if something is off. We are trained to pick up on signs of bullying, abuse, stress, depression. I thank God that I'm interactive with these kids, as I can see something you may not notice. It's very easy to be objective when they're not mine.

The next morning as I was pulling up to Emma's stop, I prayed, "God, please let her be OK."

There she stood, head of the line, with a smile on her face that would light up a runway! My heart skipped a beat seeing the joy on this child's face. She was back from the depths of sadness. She flew up the steps, greeted me warmly, and walked to her seat, where she started chattering like a magpie with Skylar. I didn't ask. I didn't bring it up. I was just so grateful she was OK.

That afternoon, Emma's mom called me on my cell phone. She wanted to thank me again for letting her know my worries about her daughter. Apparently, Mom had recently returned to work. Routine at home was disrupted, changes were happening. Mom sat Emma down for a chat. Turns out that Jordan was really being nasty to her. Jordan was also having trouble adjusting to both parents working, and her frustrations turned to Emma. The family unit sat together and tried to find a resolution.

Communication is so, so important. I'm grateful this situation ended happily. It's not to say that there was never any more squabbling between the sisters, but now the parents were more in tune with their girls. It's so hard to see what's right in front of us sometimes. Can't see the forest for the trees! I'm so blessed that Emma's mom was willing to work with me on this. She could have told me to mind my business, but she didn't. Thank you!

CHAPTER FOUR

FAITH ON THE BUS

I hail from generations of French Catholics. I was reared and schooled in the Catholic system. I made my first communion in grade two and my confirmation in grade six. I was an altar girl for two years and helped serve the 6:00 a.m. (that's right, 6:00 a.m.) mass from Monday to Saturday at our local church. It was quite a walk in the morning, but I enjoyed it. Those were the days when a young child could walk outside without worry. Every Saturday morning the parish priest would hand me six shiny dimes for my duties. Do you have any idea how much candy you could buy with sixty cents? Penny candy was five for a penny!

Two of my teachers were nuns—awesome women. I loved them, and I loved my religious studies classes. I briefly thought I might like to be a nun someday, but that phase passed. I no longer practise my Christian faith in the Catholic church. I believe the school system, although not perfect, is a good one. The difference between a faith-based school system and the public system that I work for is GOD!

You can't pray in the public school; the Lord's prayer was thrown out for fear of offending someone who is not a believer. There are no religious studies in a public school system, so some children who have no teachings at home know nothing about God. They know all about the Easter Bunny and Santa Clause, but they don't know the reason behind the season. So sad.

While I'm not told explicitly that I can't discuss my faith and my beliefs, I'm not encouraged to do so either. I will never push or bombard you with my faith, but neither will I deny it to make you comfortable. We live in such a fragile, delicate world. We constantly have to be aware of being politically correct on everything and everybody. Some days I feel we should all just wrap ourselves up in bubble wrap so we don't hurt anybody's feelings. I respect the fact that you have your opinions and values. Please allow me mine without the guilt trip. The great thing about being Canadian is that we are free! We have the right to pray to our God. Nobody, but nobody, can take that away from me. Yet that's not true anymore, is it? More and more, my faith is being pushed out of learning institutes, such as schools, and a variety of different activities, including athletics. Many organizations don't want to step on toes for fear of turning people away. I really do have a point I'm trying to get to. Sometimes I just go off on a tangent.

Ground was broken for a new school right next to the school I drive to. It would be a brand-new Catholic school, which was needed in the community. The year it opened, we saw a loss of students from our buses. Quite a few families transferred their kids over to the new school. I lost a half a dozen from my bus.

It's wonderful that we have the choice as to where to educate our children. So many countries are not as fortunate. We should never take this for granted.

We were nearing our spring break in mid-February. It had been a long winter with terrible road conditions: ice, snow, and very cold. Everybody was looking forward to a week off. A few of the kids on the bus were talking about their upcoming trips. Some were going to Mexico, and some were off to Hawaii. One family was going to Vancouver. I was just looking forward to down time and quiet time with a good book.

The last day before our break was to start, Emma got on the bus. She was bouncing because she was so excited. She couldn't hold back; she just had to tell someone, and right now! She'd just found out that she was going to New York City! I said, "New York City?" (I know, it sounds like a bad commercial.) She explained that she and her family were going to her auntie's house in New York because she, Emma, was going to be baptized.

Now please try to imagine if you can ... Emma is a wonderful little performer. She was so joyous as she told me this, and all the students within hearing range stopped what they were doing to hear it. She is a natural diva. I said, "Wow! Emma, that's awesome." I was struck then about proper conversation. Should I explore this with her? Could I? Everybody at this point was mute, like they were holding their breath to see what I would say. I said a silent prayer to God, asking him to guide me in these new waters. I did not want to mess this up. Religion is such a sensitive matter. I knew that whatever I said would be heard by all the students. I'm not bragging or boasting, but as an authority figure, I'm aware that I have influence over how kids react. I have built a rapport with these kids and believe they trust me in what I say and do. The next few minutes could really affect how and what they thought about religion. I know I'm not that powerful, but I wanted to make sure I said the right thing.

I asked Emma if she knew what baptism meant. She replied that she believed that Jesus Christ died for our sins, and she wanted to have him in her life. You could hear a pin drop on the bus. I looked at this precious, precious child of God and told her that I had been baptized two years ago in Calgary. I told her that I had given my life to Christ when I went on a mission trip to Nicaragua in 2013, and that I was so happy and proud of her. She took her seat, where she was questioned by many of her peers. They wanted to know what was going to happen, how she felt, and if it was true that she would be drowned (this from a grade one student). It was the most rewarding and loving day of my driving career.

༺∞༻

The school year was coming to a close. Students were getting itchy to be done for the summer, and teachers and bus drivers were right behind them. It was a time to say goodbye to them, but I would be back next year.

The last week of school was soon upon us. You could feel the energy, the barely contained giddiness exuding from these kids. I arrived at Emma's stop. She got on the bus, crying. Sobbing. I right away thought Jordan was bugging her. We're told as bus drivers that it's a very thin line when it comes to comforting a child. In this day and age, we have to be so careful as to our conduct with kids. I'm sorry, but when a little girl gets on my bus with tears running down her face and heaving great sobs, I'm not just going to tell her to sit down. I held my arms out to her, and she grabbed on to me right away. I patted her back and tried to quiet her. I said, "Emma, sweetheart, what is so bad in your little life that has you so upset?"

She told me through her tears and hiccupping that she would be going to the new school next year, and she wouldn't be on my bus!

My heart broke! I was stunned. I didn't see that coming, but I should have. She had been baptized, and her family was going to church with her. I should have been rejoicing for her, but I was sad with her. I told her that she'd just be next door to our school and would still be in the same neighbourhood, as always. She was just going to a new school. I told her that as scary as it might seem to go to a whole new school, she was such an awesome, super girl she'd have no problems fitting in. She'd probably already know some students who were going there. As it turned out, Skylar was there. She'd be on a different bus, but by now she was an old hand at this. I hugged her and held her tight and told her that God had given me a gift when she came on my bus. I would always think of her. She was such a blessing to me during my first year of driving. I learned so much from that little person. I hope she always stands up for herself, always says what's on her mind, and always feels the love of God shining within. God bless you, Emma.

It might be selfish of me, but I hope when she gets on her new bus, she calls her new bus driver Brenda for a few days! Is that wrong?

I believe in my heart that God placed Emma on my bus and in my life to teach me how to communicate, how to be, how to listen, how to talk to and with, and how to laugh with and at self. I was ready for her. God allowed it. Thank you, Emma!

CHAPTER FIVE

OUR LITTLE BUSING COMPANY

The Foothills School Division, which I work for, is a big operation. Mine is but one of seventy bus routes that serve the Foothills area. All together, we deliver our students to nineteen different schools and three Hutterite colonies. There are approximately 8,200 students in the area, of which close to 4,000 take the bus. We cover a combined total of 2.3 million kilometres a year. That's a lot of driving!

There is no way on God's green earth we could operate this business as smoothly as we do without our frontline office personnel! They are the driving force behind it (pun intended).

Wanda is our boss lady, and it falls to her to deal with all the higher ups in the division in regard to budget, overseeing all the routes and staff, and at times unclogging the toilets in the office. She's a force to contend with, but we'd be lost without her. She has an open-door policy, which I have used, and she's a very fair and compassionate lady to work with.

Debbie is our go-to know-it-all-and-where-everything-is lady. She works tirelessly compiling and computing all the information pertaining to four thousand students: where they live, what route they're on, and the easiest point from a to b. She's constantly updating and revising info to pass on to us drivers. She is indispensable to us.

Sandy is our dispatch queen! Hers is the voice you hear on the radio. Anything or anytime, Sandy is there to talk to you. Whether you're in a crisis, having a mechanical or discipline issue on the bus, or you're in the ditch, Sandy is the voice of reason. She is at all times calm, cool, and collected. I really can't recall ever hearing her ruffled. She has helped me immensely a couple of times during stressful situations. She talks you off the ledge and guides you back onto the road. I've heard her handle many different scenarios that are going on all at once. She will do a triage and go with the most important one at the time. She will announce for everybody to stay off the air and do what she does best. She'll either send out the tow truck, fire truck, or at times the ambulance. She won't leave you hanging; she's with you untill the situation is resolved. As drivers, we can just sit back and listen to what's going on. Her calming voice reaches across the air waves, and we can all rest easier for it.

We also have in our little family five top-notch mechanics. These guys could all work for a pit crew in NASCAR. They are awesome. They're our road angels when we've slid in the ditch, when our batteries are dead, or when warning lights are going off on the bus. Flat tires, coolant leaking, any and all glitches. Our guys have our backs. Safety first with them. They're right on top of our semi-annual inspections and our routine checks. Nothing escapes them. Because of them, we are as safe as we can be on the road.

Liseanne is our safety officer and driver trainer. She drove bus for close to twenty years and is now dedicated to driver training and safety. She trained me when I started. It's because of her incredible training that I'm confident behind the wheel. She teaches in class as well as on the road.

The first day I was to ride the bus, I was sure there was no way I'd be able to do it. It was huge! Over the many weeks of training with her, I became more comfortable. I now have eight years experience and am a better driver. I still go back to her teachings when I'm driving. I believe it has made me a better driver in my own vehicle as well.

We also take our First Aid and CPR courses with Liseanne. She's a licensed trainer for these programs. We re-certify every three years and also take fire and safety courses on a rotational basis. We must also pass our driving road test every three years to maintain our Class 2 license. Along with these mandatory programs, we attend different seminars and conferences throughout the year on our scheduled PD days. These are very informative and helpful. We get together with the teachers on these days and break into different groups that we sign up for. The topics range from how to deal with a stressful situation with students to bullying, communicating with our students, and being aware of danger.

I've come to realize that there is more to driving a school bus than meets the eye. When I get behind that wheel, I'm sitting in a huge piece of metal and glass. I start my morning every day with a pre-trip around and in my bus. I check everything from lights to tires. I check my fluids, brakes, and alarms. I check all my emergency exits, windows, and doors. If anything is amiss, it will be reported. I'll get a spare bus if it's not safe to use my bus. The lives of your children depend on me checking my bus. Complacency is the precursor to disaster!

If I'm not feeling up to snuff, or I'm fighting something like the flu, I'm not operating at 100 per cent. We've been told that if we're not comfortable driving in a situation, we won't be forced to. I had a gall bladder attack a couple of years ago and had to call in at 6:00 a.m. to let the office know I couldn't go in. I'm very fortunate that I have a healthy disposition. I catch the odd cold from the kids, usually in October, for just a couple of days. I make sure to keep disinfectant wipes on the bus, and I try to wipe down the railing, but sometimes you just get what they pass around. It hasn't stopped me from driving. I just let them know that they did this to me. They don't really care.

As drivers, we face all kinds of different scenarios on any given day. The worst is in the winter months. Driving conditions can be horrendous! We've had a few snow days since I've been working. The division decides whether the roads are a safety hazard to drivers, and they will call it. Kids love it. I've driven in some hairy snowy, icy conditions. My fingers were sore from gripping the steering wheel, and when I got back to the compound, I had to remember to breathe. I always thank God for keeping us all safe.

On particularly bad days, we listen carefully to the radio to find out from other drivers about accidents ahead, road closures, or someone in the ditch. In these situations, we rally around each other. Someone might have slid into the ditch with a load of students on board. We start radioing each other to get to the stranded bus driver. We figure out who's closest and who has room on their bus. The students will be picked up and driven home while the boys come with the tow truck. It all comes down to communication and working together as a team. Nobody gets left behind. We work as a unit. We have to ensure the safety of our kids and our drivers.

Aside from weather conditions, the worst infraction out there is other drivers. I'm not allowed to go over ninety kilometres and hour. I have a big sticker on my back side that lets you know that. I know that people don't want to be stuck behind me on the highway, but that's the law. I'm sure they think their time is more important than mine when I'm at a stop to pick up the students, and my lights are flashing and my big stop sign is out. They obviously see the kids standing there, yet they don't feel that they should have to wait the ninety seconds it will take to load the kids. I have the kids get on the bus as quickly and safely as possible. I don't sit there with the lights on just to annoy the waiting drivers. But they decide their time is much more important, so they ignore my lights. I see them coming and tap my horn to let them know, but they keep advancing. I might have stragglers running for the bus, but still these impatient drivers keep coming. They don't want to be inconvenienced by the big yellow bus in front of them. Again, I tap the horn a little more forcefully this time. They actually hesitate for a fraction of a second. My kids all freeze. They know that when I'm hitting the horn, someone is driving through our lights. Had the police been there, the offender would have received a $500.00 fine and five demerits for crossing a school bus with lights flashing. As it is, I take down the license plate numbers and fill in the forms that I keep on my bus. I then bring them to the RCMP division, who will in turn check it out and issue a ticket to the registered owner.

I've placed many complaints with the RCMP over the years. I've even had to go to court because some people are quite offended that I would squeal on them. They have the option to plead not guilty in court. I'm always prepared to testify when I'm served with a subpoena. I've never had to because they've always pleaded guilty when they see that I am there. The safety of my students is much more important than whatever is so pressing that warrants not stopping for the school bus. It is so infuriating when I see this happening time and time again. I see them driving and texting while coming toward me. They don't even realize that they're swerving a little into my lane. I have to have eyes all over the place. I'm watching them not watching me, and I'm looking behind me in case I have to stop. I'm mindful of that deer on the side of the road, and there is the oncoming vehicle, oblivious to the surroundings. I'm constantly on alert. I have to be on the defensive at all times, for any given situation that might occur.

I take my duties as a bus driver very seriously. It's not just a job with lots of time off. The children on my bus trust that I will get them to school and back home safely. Their parents feel that way too. By the time summer break is here, every bus driver in the world is breathing a sigh of relief. We have survived another year. God willing, it was a safe one. That's all we can ask for. When you see the big yellow nuisance with the lights flashing, warning you to stop, PLEASE STOP! You don't want to see me when I'm mad!

A sign in our training office reads: "HONK IF YOU LOVE JESUS. DRIVE AND TEXT IF YOU WANT TO MEET HIM RIGHT NOW!"

CHAPTER SIX

ARE YOU HAVING FUN YET?

When I get to heaven and God asks me if I had fun on earth, I want to be able to say, "You betcha! I had a blast! Thank you."

It's unrealistic and a little worrisome to think that every day is going to be butterflies and balloons. It's not! But I find as I travel on my journey with God, my days are so much livelier and joyful. I am genuinely having fun. I enjoy children today. Of course, it's much easier to enjoy and tolerate other people's children. I'm a wonderful aunt to my sister's daughter. She thinks I'm awesome and really cool. I get to spoil her and have fun with her and commiserate with her about her mother. She's twenty-five now and a beautiful young woman. I really think if we could skip parenthood and go right to being grandparents, everybody would be soooo happy. Just think about it for a minute … we wouldn't have the pressure of raising children to grow up to be upstanding members of society. We could just spoil them and not have to worry about feeding them chocolate cake for supper. We'd lose the stress of raising them properly and to have it better than we did. We need to educate them and then worry when their grades aren't so good. Will they be able to get a job when they're older? Will they be well adjusted and happy? Will they be in good health? Will they need braces? Will they find love and marriage? The list goes on and on! When you're a grandparent, your stress is done. Your job is to enjoy them and then send them back home. Your job is done.

I think that's why I enjoy driving the bus so much. I can have a relationship with these awesome kids and then you get them back. They think I'm a great bus driver (they've told me so), but I don't have to take them home with me. When I call you the week before school starts to confirm that your child will be on the bus and to let you know what time I'll be picking them up, you can't hide the joy in your voice. You are so ready to send them back to me on the bus! By then, I'm ready to have them back. I'm recharged and reenergized. I'm ready for another year with these awesome little creatures.

The children on my bus range from Kindergarten to grade twelve. Every one of them is so unique and of their own mind. I've learned so much from each and every one of them, from the babies to the high schoolers. To do so, I have to get down to their level. Again, it's so much easier to do this with somebody else's child.

I was eighteen when they placed my newborn daughter in my arms. I was terrified! I had no clue whatsoever about this little thing. It took me eight diapers to finally get one on her the first time I attempted to change her. I was planning on breastfeeding her, so I would lock myself in my room, hold her out at arm's length, and tell her, "OK, go ahead and feed." Luckily, I was staying with my mother at that time. I left my daughter's father in California and came home five months pregnant. Had it not been for my mother, I wouldn't have survived, nor would my daughter, who is now a grandmother herself.

Two weeks after she was born, I returned to the hospital and asked to speak to a nurse. I explained that I hadn't received the bonding box. She asked me what I was talking about. I said, "You know, the box that comes with the baby that makes you bond with her! I didn't receive it." I was so young, so unprepared for motherhood. I really thought it would be a piece of cake, a lark. I thought I could use cloth diapers and breastfeed for two years and it wouldn't cost me a fortune. So, so naïve! Well, as I said, she survived. More luck than management on my part. If you ask my daughter, she'll tell you I was a wonderful mother. I made a lot of mistakes, and many tears were shed (mine), but she seems to have come out in one piece. She's a better mother to her children than I was to her, which is why I seriously think if we all skipped parenthood and went right to being grandma, we'd all be better equipped to handle things.

To me, raising her was such a HUGE responsibility. I was so afraid of making any mistakes. I couldn't enjoy her for fear of messing things up. I didn't how to just have fun with her. All of a sudden, I had to be grown up and look after this tiny little girl who relied on me for her very life. That is scary! What if I broke her? What if she didn't like me? What if I made her cry? So many what ifs. God doesn't make mistakes! I received the help I needed to care for my daughter. She had the best grandmother in the world. My mother doted on her first grandchild. She enjoyed her so much; she thought the sun rose and set on her. My daughter adored her grandmother and grandfather immensely. The bond they shared lasted till the day my mother passed away in August 2016. I didn't have a good relationship with my mother, but I believe she poured all her love onto my daughter as a means to make up for that. Thank you, Mom.

I always felt so awkward around children; I didn't know what to do with them. I couldn't see them as real little people. They were like another species, totally different. They had their own language, and I didn't understand them. To be perfectly honest, I was intimidated and terrified of them, so I stayed away from them. I come from the era of "Children should be seen and not heard." My parents didn't have time to enjoy us kids; we were a responsibility and a job. They were there to feed us and clothe us, but children were not fun. They nurtured us, they loved us, they protected us, but that was their job. And they did it to the best of their ability. They had a hard life, my folks. We didn't have much, but they worked hard and raised us. We always had food on the table, and they would do as much as they could with the little, they had. We were their children, not their friends or peers! That's just the way it was.

I grew up with discipline and rules. I grew up with spankings and punishments. Sometimes they were quite harsh, but I believe I am who I am today as a result of my upbringing. I have work ethics and values today as a direct result of my childhood. There is so much lacking today in the form of manners and discipline in the home. I don't advocate abuse of a child, but I also don't agree that Johnny should be able to run the household or that time-outs are an answer to everything. My daughter will tell you that she received about five spankings in her life. She'll also tell you she deserved them all and then some.

W.C. Fields was once asked during an interview how he liked children. He replied, "Barbequed!" That's hilarious. Of course, saying that today could put you in hot water.

I have fun on the bus. I don't know if the kids do, but I do. I love laughing with them, hearing them laugh, and laughing at them. I celebrate birthdays on my bus. Once a month I find out who has a birthday in the next month, and they get a special treat and a rousing rendition from everyone on the bus of "Happy Birthday." I also decorate the bus for different occasions, such as Valentine's Day, St. Patrick's Day, Halloween, and Christmas. The kids seem to enjoy it. One year, I decided not to decorate for Halloween, as it fell on the weekend. Nothing was mentioned. The next year, Ava, who would have been in grade four at that time, stopped by my seat before getting off the bus and asked if I was going to decorate the bus that year for Halloween. I asked if she would like me to, and she and quite a few others boisterously replied, "YES!" So I dug out my supply of decorations, bought more, and had a blast doing up the bus for them. They were squealing and shrieking when they got on the next day. It takes so little to make them happy. The idea that I followed through for them was all they wanted.

April Fools' Day is a fun day on the bus. Some of my students are too savvy to fall for tricks, but the ones that do are hilarious. I've pulled off a couple of good capers over the years, one of which was to convince the students that Justin Bieber was to perform a concert at their school! Grades four and five girls were not impressed! Another year, I had the bus convinced that we had won a super prize for being the bus that was the most knowledgeable about bus safety and our regular drills. I told them the prize was an overnight trip to West Edmonton Mall.

My bus is relatively quiet, considering I have between fifty and sixty kids on it at any given time. If they do get a little loud, I just ask them to turn it down a bit, which they do. They know that I have to hear the dispatcher if she comes on the air. I have a radio on the bus, but I find that too distracting on top of watching all the traffic and the kids and everything around me. I prefer just the noise of the students. Every once in a while, I'm astounded at how quiet a busload of kids can be, and I actually check my mirror to make sure they're on the bus. They're all just chatting quietly amongst themselves, peaceful, serene. Then *bam*! Kaliyah, my little grade one girl, screams at the top of her lungs (keep in mind she sits right behind me) "HOLY COW! Look at that sky! It's beautiful!" As I peel myself off the ceiling and try to get my heart rate back under three hundred, I glance over to the west, and, yes, the sky is beautiful. The Rocky Mountains in the background, the incredible blue sky, and a hint of a remaining rainbow. Thank you for sharing that, Kaliyah! Through the eyes of a child, I have seen so much. The beauty that surrounds me is new again. I don't want to lose sight of that. We need to be childlike in order to come to God. What better way than to observe the little ones.

There are thirty windows on my bus, as well as my huge windshield. When the sun hits the bus, it can be like a greenhouse effect in there. I have a roof hatch that I open, which helps as we're going down the road. I usually open a few windows when I leave the bus compound in the afternoon in the hopes of cooling down the bus. It can get so hot in there some days. I've had a couple of students suffer nosebleeds because of the heat. A couple of years ago, I brought a spray bottle from home, filled with water. As the kids load on the bus, I stand outside and they put their hands up, glasses off, and I spray away. I soak their heads and down the back of their shirts. They absolutely love it! If they let me know that they don't want to be sprayed, I respect that. No means no. There are plenty who want to be sprayed. I even have other kids and their parents who walk by my bus asking if they can get sprayed. I always share. When I'm back on the bus with about two minutes till we leave, I walk up and down the aisle spraying as many as I can. The rule is, if you want to be sprayed, put your hands up. The ride home is so much more comfortable for them all. It's refreshing and fun. I've had some kids ask me to spray them right in the face, eyes closed, mouth open!

Every once in a while, it gets really quiet on the bus ride home in the afternoon. As I'm about to pull up to one of the stops, I'll yell out, "Girls rule boys drool." That gets them going! They're still nattering as they're getting off the bus.

CHAPTER SEVEN

FROM THE MOUTH OF BABES

When my daughter was around three years old, I realized just how my mother's words were so true. She used to tell me that "little pitchers had big ears." Children are mimics! What you say and do is absorbed by them, secreted away, and taken out when it's to their advantage. I don't even know if they're aware of what they're doing. My daughter was being a typical three-year-old on this particular day. I had reached my limit and sent her to her room. As she was heading up the stairs to her bedroom, I realized that I needed something from my room. Unbeknownst to her, I was right behind her on the stairs. She didn't hear me. As she got to the landing, she put her hands on her hips, starting shaking her head and her hips, and in a voice that I can only imagine was a loose rendition of mine, started yapping, "You get to your room right now, young lady!" I clamped my hand over my mouth for fear she would hear me laugh. I turned right around without a sound and went back downstairs. She was hilarious! I didn't dare let her know that I'd seen her. But from then on, I was so aware of how little people are aware of everything.

Never underestimate this species! They know all and see all. They truly are innocents. They spurt out whatever they're thinking at the moment. They don't have a filter like we do. They don't have to stop and wonder if what they're about to say is offensive or wrong or incorrect. I don't think they consciously mean to be rude or cruel. They just don't know. It's we adults that are marred by the ugliness around us. We lash out at the world and are fearful of its state. We feel powerless. To be a child, to be free of constraints, to not worry about every single issue and where you stand on it, is wonderful. Can you pay the bills this month? Will you keep your job? Will the economy turn around? Will your family survive? In Canada, for the most part, our children are free to be children and don't need to ask these questions. We have homeless families in our cities, and we have hungry children, but we have so much more freedom in our country. We have different avenues to help us, such as health care, social services, and government funding. We thankfully can still let our children be children. They're not put out to war like in some countries. They can run freely, play in the streets, and pray in the churches of their choice. I thank God I am Canadian!

I don't realize how much my kids are taking in until something I've said to them comes back to me. They are so nonchalant about their time on the bus. It's a daily part of their routine, and not much changes. They get on, sit for a bit, then get off. Once in a while, I'll get a call from my dispatch advising me that one of my students is going to have a friend on the bus for the trip home. We have to account for these extra riders in case of any emergency; we need to know who is on the bus. I've never had a problem with guest riders. They get on and introduce themselves and then go sit with their friend. There's an area on my route that runs around the golf course. It's a one-way, narrow road, and the trees bordering it are huge. Depending on the time of year, the branches hang down heavily. Often, they scrape the roof of my bus. It sounds like a thousand squirrels running across the top. My kids are used to it and don't even comment on it anymore. When we have a guest rider and this happens, the newcomer will shout out, "What was that?" A group of students will yell out, "Trimming trees!" That explains everything, and we carry on. I just grin and drive. At other times when we have a guest rider, if I notice a vehicle coming through my area with my lights flashing as the students are unloading, I'll tap the horn. If the driver continues to come forward, I honk the horn. My kids know to freeze till I have this situation under control. I don't know if this person is going to stop, and I don't want my kids in harm's way. A guest rider will usually ask what's going on, and a chorus of kids will yell out, "Some fool is crossing our lights!" I was shocked the first time I heard this coming from them. I didn't realize how much they picked up from me.

When I first started driving bus, I signed up for field trips. These are extra hours for us bus drivers and can be beneficial. We get to go to the zoo and different parks and events. We get paid over and above our regular hours. The downfall of this is that we get somebody else's kids. I may get a trip to the zoo with fifty kids on board. There might be a half a dozen that are mine. There's usually a couple of teachers or parent chaperones along. The kids are wild; it's like they've never been out before. It can get very loud, depending on if the teachers are keeping an eye out. I'm checking my mirror and end up telling a few to sit down and face front. My kids don't act like that. As a matter of fact, when mine are on these field trips, they're so excited that they get to be on their own bus. They love showing off their bus, their bus driver, their seat. It's a big deal to them. They have status here. I always make sure to chat with them as they get on the bus. Wow! The bus driver knows them. And they're very quick to tell the students around them that there is no eating on their bus, and they had better not litter. There's a garbage can up front. They're proud of our clean bus. I get a lump in my throat when I hear them proudly displaying their name tags by their seats and pointing out our decorations. Yeah, they're so cool. I don't take field trips anymore. There aren't that many at our school, and I prefer to drive the kids I know.

It felt good to know my kids were happy to see me when I did the field trips. Every once in a while, they ask if I'm driving on the upcoming trip they're going on next week. I tell them, "No, I only drive you guys because, I only like you guys." That's good enough for them.

CHAPTER EIGHT

ODDS AND SODS

Throughout the school year, we get new students on our bus who have just moved to the area. On these occasions, we're asked to call the new parents and chat with them. I received a call from the office one day letting me know I would have a new kindergartener starting the following week. I phoned the mom and introduced myself as her son's bus driver. I asked if he had any allergies that I should be aware of, and if she had any questions. This was a brand-new experience for her five-year-old, Cannon. I assured her I'd take good care of him, and that I'd see her at the allocated bus stop Monday morning. Before we hung up, she told me I should have no problem recognizing Cannon, as he was very big for his age. I said I'd look out for him, and she again said that he was very big, so I wouldn't miss him.

Come Monday morning, as I was about to pull up to her stop, I reminded myself to look for our new student amidst the group of twenty-five or so kids. I need not have worried about missing him. He was very big indeed! As the students were loading, Cannon and his mom waited to get on last. I said hi to Mom and pointed to the first seat up front for Cannon to sit. Meanwhile, Mom was taking pictures of him walking up the stairs, turning around, and waving at her. She was jumping around trying to take pictures of him sitting. I finally asked her to step on the bus and take a picture of him in his seat (I already had his name tag up). Then she could go. She was beaming! Cannon was very comfortable and very chatty. I learned all about where he came from in Texas, what his dad did for a living, the fact that he had two younger brothers at home, and his favourite pastimes. All this in about twelve minutes. He fit right in with our little bus family.

The Christmas concert was just around the corner, and the kids were getting excited. I lost count of how many renditions of "Frosty the Snowman" and "Rudolph the Red-Nosed Reindeer" I had to listen to. Emma, my sweet girl, got on the bus one afternoon and let out a heavy sigh as she sat down. I asked her what was up, and she said that the Christmas concert was the next day, and she just wished her mom didn't have to work. Mom wasn't going to be able to make it. My heart broke for this child. She lived in a beautiful home in an affluent neighbourhood and didn't lack for much. But her mom had to work the night of her concert. She was so sad. The importance we place on our work, as seen through the eyes of our little ones, can be everlasting. They don't understand that we so want to be there for them at all times, but sometimes we just can't. I couldn't chaperone at my daughter's school, as I always worked. I know it bothered her that I couldn't be there, but as adults we have responsibilities that have to be met. I did get involved where and when I could through her Girl Guides group and other extra-curricular activities. I knew how Emma was feeling, and I also knew how her mom must have been feeling. We as parents just want to shelter our kids from all kinds of hurt and disappointments.

I have a seating arrangement on my bus, both for safety reasons and for order on the bus. The kids like to know where they sit, as it gives them a sense of consistency and security. They belong here. I try to pair them up with someone they get along with, such as a classmate or neighbour. The first couple of weeks of school I draw out a rough draft of the seating plan. If some students desperately want to sit with someone in particular, I try to accommodate them. Depending on how many of each grade I have, at times I have to sit different grades together. For the most part, it works out. Not surprisingly, the students will come up to me after a couple of weeks and ask if they can sit with somebody else. I allow this once in a while. There are some students, however, who don't seem to do well with anybody. It seems that every other week they want to change seat mate. When this starts, I have a dozen other kids who want to sit with somebody else. This can be frustrating and very time consuming! The fact that they're on the bus for maybe twenty minutes in the morning and maybe fifteen in the afternoon means that it shouldn't be a big deal to sit with so and so. I'd finally had enough of constantly changing names around! I announced a couple of years ago that we would not be changing seats again. Who you are with is who you will be sitting with for the year, unless there was a really good reason to sit somewhere else. They groaned and complained as kids do, but I did announce that I was now implementing a new rule. Every Friday afternoon would be considered Free Friday! On this day, they could sit with whoever they wanted, wherever they wanted—except for the very last two seats, which we keep for the older students. In case of emergency, they need to be ready to assist at the back. In return for allowing this, I didn't want to hear them asking if they could sit with so and so during the week. They still ask if they can sit with a friend, and all I ask is "Is it Friday?" They look forward to Fridays, and they get on the bus yelling "Free Friday!" We have to amend this rule when there's no school on a Friday, and we make it Free Thursday. They are sticklers to this rule! The odd time that I've had to take time off, I warn the sub driver of this rule. One was convinced the kids were making this up, kind of like when you tell the babysitter that you're allowed cake instead of supper. I assured him it was true.

There is a little playground area on my bus route. I drop off kids near to it. One day as we were driving by, I noticed that one of the pieces of equipment was all covered up. I asked Alex what that was about. He replied that the seesaw was broken, and it was going to be taken away and fixed. I thought that was the end of the conversation. No! Alex, who was in grade three at that time, informed me that he "got his balls cracked on that thing!" If I had false teeth, I would have spit them out. As it was, I chocked out, "What?"

He thought I hadn't heard him, when in reality I was just shocked by his response. He repeated his answer. "Yeah, that thing cracked my balls." He said it like he was talking about the weather. It wasn't a big deal. This is a perfectly normal thing to say to your bus driver. Oh my gosh! I raised a little girl! She didn't talk like that. I sputtered out that hopefully the seesaw would be fixed soon. I then opened the door at his stop and wished him a good night. He didn't see anything wrong with his observation; he was just stating facts.

Every bus driver has their own way of doing things. We all have basic rules of the bus. Sit in your seat on your bum. Face forward. Nothing in the aisles. Keep the noise level to a dull roar. On my bus, I don't allow eating. Rules are necessary in the home as well as on the bus. I need to maintain order on my bus when I'm driving, as I'm concentrating on the road, the traffic, and other vehicles all around. I don't want to have to worry about my kids running around and getting into trouble. They know what's expected of them, and for the most part they're very well behaved. Over the years, I've added a few rules to the bus, which may or may not be followed.

Brenda's Bus Commandments!

1) Never, ever, under any circumstance, anytime, anywhere within the walls of this bus, are you to sing "The wheels on the bus go round and round." EVER.
2) No Christmas songs before December 1 or after January 1. Period. No discussion. I can't take thirty different renditions of "Rudolph" in such closed quarters. Bah humbug!
3) No licking the windows! Really? Do I need to explain why? I only have so many Lysol wipes to go around.
4) No licking your seat mate either.
5) No writing "Help Me" backwards in the frosted window. That's not funny! I get such weird looks from other drivers.
6) No tossing your brother out the window. I don't care what he's done to you.
7) As stated in an earlier chapter, no picking anybody else's nose.
8) No asking how old the bus driver is and then looking at me like I'm a little old lady.
9) Absolutely no farting on your way off the bus, especially when the heaters are on. You stink!
10) No more then three renditions of "Guess What, Chicken-butt?" per week.
11) No screaming hysterically because there's a wasp on the bus. It brings on a rippling effect. Chris is the only one who has allergies to wasps, and you don't hear him screaming. Ummm, could someone check on Chris? He's pretty quiet.

CHAPTER NINE

U-TURNS

I admire people who can look at the night sky and find their way home by the stars.

I'm in awe of people who can tell what direction they're facing at any given time.

I'm amazed at people who can use a compass!

I'm envious of people who can read a map.

God has a sense of humour. My brain is not wired to compute directional navigation. Therefore, people are always telling where to go! Seriously, I get lost in my own back yard. I have no sense at all when it comes to where I am. I once saw a wall mural (can't remember where) of a child walking down a country lane surrounded by trees on both sides. It was a beautiful sunny day for a walk. The caption above read, "I don't know where I'm going, but I'm on my way!" That is so me! Talk about faith. As long as

I have God in my life, it doesn't really matter where I go. I know I'll be safe.

I used to get so frustrated at my lack of direction. My husband, Jim, is a very patient man. When I call and ask for directions, he calmly sets me on the right path again. I get lost with a GPS in my vehicle. I second guess it, as obviously it doesn't know it all!

An Indigenous lady once tried to teach me the ways to tell which direction I was facing. I know the mountains are in the west. That's it. She talked about seeing where the sun was in the sky, moss on the trees, different things that might help me navigate a little easier. So, I asked her how I could tell which way I was facing if I was in the middle of Saskatchewan, it's an overcast day, with no mountains or trees. How do I tell? She replied, "What are you doing in Saskatchewan?"

I was a late bloomer when it came to driving. I was twenty-five before I got my license. I felt no need for it, living in Calgary. I used the transit system to get around. I enrolled in an AMA driving course, got my license, and bought my first car—a blue 1977 Ford Pinto station wagon. It was the 1976 models that blew up. Just saying. It had a blue shag interior, new paint job, and a full tank of gas. I paid $1500.00 for it. I loved that car. Got many speeding tickets in that car. I got lost quite a bit in that car. I would drive up 16 Avenue in Calgary, and when I'd pass the travel info centre, I'd turn around because I knew I was going the wrong way again. I would get so upset with myself. I just couldn't get it through my noggin East from West and South from North. I would joke that as I passed the info centre, the little guy who worked in there would come out and wave at me to let me know I was going in the wrong direction.

Maybe it's the fear of getting lost that makes me very anxious about being on time. I would rather be twenty minutes early than five minutes late. I grew up in a family that had no regard for timetables. They were on their own schedule. This would drive (See the pun?) me crazy. I find it so rude and inconsiderate of my time when I'm left waiting. Sure, things happen, but with my family, it was almost like they relished being late. They didn't really see a problem with it. Get over it. So maybe I obsess about it. If I have to go somewhere I've never been, I like to map out (I'm just full of puns today.) exactly where I'm going. I feel anxious and nervous until I reach my destination. I allow plenty of time for fear (reality) of getting lost. I just input an extra fifteen minutes for the inevitable. I'm sure some of you reading this probably think I'm exaggerating. Really, I'm not. I have gotten better over the years. GPS is a wonderful aid for the most part. Bluetooth in my truck is very helpful also when I call Jim and blather that I'm lost again. I really think this is a lesson in humility God is trying to teach me. JUST ASK FOR DIRECTIONS. Why is it so hard to ask for help? I usually wait till I'm so far off the beaten track before I admit complete defeat. God has me exactly where he wants me. And for this, I am very grateful.

When I was hired as a bus driver, I was a spare. This means that wherever I was needed, I was to go. I could be in Okotoks today and Priddis tomorrow. I might be in Black Diamond for a week or High River for two days. As a spare, you're up for anything. You're given a map and a diagram of where to go.

1) I don't do well with maps.
2) Diagrams are even worse.

This is where the grace of God comes in. I was hired in July of 2013 and was given a map of the area I'd be driving. I was told that I was to be a spare on this route for a little while. The route was actually being held for a driver who was on sick leave. How long she'd be out, we didn't know. For the time being, I would only have to do this route. I thank my driver trainer, Liseanne, for this. Unbeknownst to me, she mentioned to my boss at that time, Virginia, that I would make a good bus driver but would be better if I could stick to just one route. They would lose me if I were to bounce around all over the Foothills district. Some spares love the variety of driving different routes. Not for me.

For two weeks I went over and over and over again, from the first stop to the last stop, until I was confident that come the first day of school, I would not get lost. If I missed a stop, I'd start all over again from the beginning. I'm pleased to say that I didn't get lost.

I was considered a spare on this route for the full school year. At year end, the route was given to me permanently. The bus driver who was on leave was assigned a different route. Route 22 was mine for keeps. As a permanent driver, I'm entitled to the same benefits as the Alberta Teachers' Union. We get paid all year through. We're an association with excellent benefits. The fact that I never had to drive another route was a bonus. I really don't think I would have lasted if I'd had to venture out all over the place all the time—in the dead of winter, when it's dark out till 8:00 a.m., and you're on a narrow country road with snowplows nowhere to be seen, and you're trying to find your first stop. I would have probably tossed the keys out and walked home! I've been the Route 22 driver for eight full years now. I hardly ever get lost anymore! I like routine and consistency. I like knowing where I'm going, and I adapt when needed. But I feel easier when I think I have control over the situation. HAH!

The Wheels on the Bus

I was at the bus compound one day, having finished my morning route and fuelled up the bus. My fellow bus driver Jennifer was also there. We were chatting in the coffee room when our boss, Virginia, walked in and asked what we were up to for the morning. We both told her we had no plans. She asked if we'd go to Calgary and drop off some parts at a shop, pick up some parts from another location, and finally, on our return trip, one of us drive a bus back from Calgary.

Sure, we said. It would be an easy trip. We'd get paid a couple of extra hours, and we'd be in good with the boss. What could possibly go wrong? Everything ... that's what! I told the boss we could take my truck, as I had a GPS on board. She said we were to take the company truck, as it was already loaded with the parts we had to drop off. (Why didn't I think to take my GPS out of my truck?) We were given a photocopied kind of sort of map. Keep in mind that there were no addresses or business names on this map, just five red dots indicating where we were supposed to go. Piece of cake! Of course, I couldn't admit that this "map" was confusing. I figured between Jennifer and myself we'd figure it out.

We left the yard at 9:30 a.m. We had plenty of time to get all the errands done and pick up the bus. We had five hours before we had to get going for our afternoon route. RIGHT! What should have taken twenty minutes to our first destination took an hour and a half. We got so totally turned around in the industrial area in Calgary, it was very sad. We managed to drop off the parts and then proceeded to our next stop. The map was totally useless.

Meanwhile, the office was keeping tabs on us by radio dispatch. We let them know our progress, which was not much, but we still had plenty of time. I was doing the driving while Jennifer navigated. I should mention that Jennifer's sense of direction makes me look like an expert! She was worse than I could ever be. At one point we were so lost, she got on her cell phone to get directions via computer. The recorded voice came on asking where we wanted to go. Jennifer had it on speaker so I could hear the directions. The "voice" kept getting the name of the street we wanted totally wrong, and Jennifer was getting frustrated with this automaton! The fourth time she was asked to repeat the name of the street, Jennifer screamed at her phone, "That's not what I asked for!" The voice came back with, "I'm sorry, could you repeat that please." Well, Jennifer lost it. She started yelling and carrying on at this phone. I burst out laughing. I was howling. It was a combination of my fears rising from being lost and my anxiety of being late getting back. We both wanted to do well and get a pat on the shoulder from the boss.

We couldn't find the second stop, and we still had three more to do plus get the bus. It was now nearing 12:00 p.m., and we had a little under two hours before we have to head back. We were both panicking. Again, we got a call from the office to see how we were doing. I let them know that we'd hit a wall with the directions, and we were trying to get on track.

As Jennifer was arguing with the cell phone voice, I shouted at her, "You realize you're screaming to a computer?" We then both started laughing like a bunch of drunken sailors. We regrouped and talked to the office. They decided that we'd have to give up the other stops if we were to make it back in time. As for the bus we needed to pick up, it wasn't ready anyway. Soooo I headed back for home. I checked the time, and we had time to get back, get our buses, and get to the school to pick up the students. We were still OK. We both relaxed a bit. Oh well, we managed to get a couple of items the boss wanted.

Remember when I said I don't know my East from my West? I don't know which way is which? I was on the highway, making our way home, when I saw the exit. I took the ramp and was rocking down the road. A few minutes later, Jennifer said, "Are we going the right way?" I assured her we were. A few minutes later, she said, "Brenda, where are the mountains?" I asked her what she was talking about. She answered, "Shouldn't we be seeing the mountains if we're heading home?"

At that exact moment, the office radioed us to ask how we were doing. I told them we were just coming on to Indus. The boss very calmly asked if I had just said Indus, and I said, "Yep, we're on our way back." Virginia was an awesome lady—very patient, very calming. She had worked for the transportation department for close to thirty-five years. She'd started out as a bus driver and over the years, with her experience and abilities, became the manager and supervisor of all the bus drivers. She was used to all aspects of the road and people. Nothing really flustered her at this stage. I don't think I ever saw her flabbergasted. She portrayed the image of confidence and strength. I was intimidated by her when I first met her … for quite a while, actually. I just so wanted to get this right.

Meanwhile, back in the truck, Jennifer was still blathering about the stupid mountains! Where were they? That's when Virginia very calmly and slowly, as if she was sneaking up on a deer and didn't want to spook it, told me I was going the wrong way! If I was seeing the sign for Indus, I should probably turn around as soon as I could. Of course, Jennifer was gloating and laughing so hard, she had tears rolling down her face: "I told you we should be seeing mountains."

ARGHHH! Now we were really cutting it close. I had a mental picture of the office personnel and all the mechanics standing around the radio to see what was going to happen next. I'm sure they were laying bets to see if we'd make it back in time. What started out as a short trip to the city was now becoming tiresome. (Did you see what I did with tire ... as in car tire?) We got turned around, and I told Jennifer I didn't want to hear a peep out of her. We got back to the yard, left the keys in the truck, and ran for our buses. We made it to the school with two minutes to spare. Oh yeah! We are good.

I avoided the office for quite a while after that. The thing about our bus radio was that all drivers knew what we were doing and got a play-by-play update. We were not spared. Our reputations were set from that day forward. About a week after this fiasco, the boss got on the radio and asked if anybody could make a trip to Calgary. I picked up my mic and offered mine and Jennifer's services. Virginia very diplomatically relayed that I was probably needed elsewhere. But thanks anyway. I still get teased about this episode. The heart is willing; the mind, however, gets lost. I have never been asked to do a part run again.

Ten buses drive out of the school where I drop off my students. The name of the school is Heritage Heights. It is a kindergarten to grade nine school and a very nice facility. All told, we deliver between 350 to 400 students. It's a well-oiled machine that gets everybody picked up and dropped off on time. This is why it's so important to keep on schedule.

The winter of 2017/2018 was horrible! There was so much snow that year. I don't mind the cold, but the snow is really hazardous at times. I have a sturdy bus, but at times snow life happens. We got a call on the radio one afternoon that one of our drivers had slid into the ditch. There was no getting out without a tow, and she still had half a dozen students on the bus. Nobody was hurt, just stuck. It would take our boys about a half an hour to forty-five minutes to reach her, as the road she was on wasn't good. They actually had to chain up their rig to get to her. Keep in mind that we're in the country here, and the plows hadn't been out yet. The roads were so heavy with snow that it was hard to differentiate the road from the ditch. Everything was white! The snow drifts were incredible.

When I heard the driver call in for a tow, I got on the radio to let the office know I was clear of my students. I was the closest to her bus, so I could go get her kids and bring them home. This is what we do. We help each other out in any given situation. We didn't want the kids on the bus for forty-five minutes till the tow truck got there. I was about six minutes out, so I headed over to her.

I carefully made my way over and loaded up her students. The kids were very good about pointing the way to where they lived. Having dropped off the last student, I radioed the office to let them know my progress and told them I was heading home. The mechanics were still making their way with the tow truck. As I said, it was so white everywhere, and I was on a narrow road where I dropped off the last student. I carried on, not realizing that I was driving in a circular roadway. Had I followed it around, I would have found my way out, but the snow had totally covered any tracks to guide me. Instead of following the circular route, I branched off to what I thought was the right direction. A few minutes of driving up this blanketed road and I came to a dead end. There was no more road! I was facing train tracks! They weren't there when I was there ten minutes earlier. I deduced that I'd obviously missed my turn somewhere and looked around for somewhere to turn around. I can only fathom what it must be like to be lost in the desert or Siberia.

The effect of the snow was almost blinding. I've heard of snow blindness and how confusing and disorienting it can be. I was on a very narrow, tree-lined country lane, not knowing where the shoulder of the road met the ditch. There were no tracks in the snow to guide me. It was very daunting! I had just passed a house and decided that if I could back up a few feet, I could position my back end in their long driveway and turn myself around and head back in the right direction. The fact that they had signs all over their property warning that trespassers would be shot did kind of worry me, but I had no choice. The road I was on was too narrow to safely navigate a U-turn. I figured my best bet would be to back into the driveway.

I proceeded to back up slowly, watching my mirrors and trying to guesstimate where the driveway was. It didn't take long to figure out I was totally off my mark. The snow was so soft and so plentiful. It would have been beautiful if I didn't have to plow through it. My back end skidded and slid right away. I put her in drive and turned the wheel, but I couldn't get traction! I reversed again and slid again. I kept turning the wheel, hoping to grab on to something, anything. It wasn't going to happen. I just kept spinning my tires.

I was faced with a decision. I could either hunker down there for the night, hoping that the landowners were just kidding about their warnings, or I could radio in and let the office know I was STUCK! I radioed in. The dispatch asked where I was. I said, "I don't know." She knew I'd dropped off the other kids, so I must be somewhere close by. I told her I'd missed the turn due to the snow. I really didn't know where I was because out there in the boondocks there were no street signs. I couldn't even see a marker or 911 address, which is what property owners in the country use.

The bus driver I'd helped got on the radio to see if she could figure out where I was. When something like this happens, dispatch will ask all bus drivers to stand by so she can help the driver in trouble. Now I had every bus driver in the district listening to me say, "I don't know where I am." Through my directional ramblings, the bus driver knew where I was. This was, after all, her area.

The guys had just arrived to tow her out, and she was able to relay to them where I should be. Due to the amount of snow and conditions of the road, I was rescued about half an hour later. I got out of my bus when they pulled up, and I saw just where I'd ended up. The snow had drifted so much that what I thought was the driveway was a steep ditch. The guys were having trouble getting in. They took it all in good stride. Love those guys. My heroes for the day. They had me hooked up and out of there within ten minutes. I felt foolish, but oh well. The end result was that everybody got home safe and sound. This wouldn't stop me from helping out again if needed.

I let dispatch know I was out and on my way home. Quite a few bus drivers got on the air and high fived me. We are a family who works together. We tease each other, we may quarrel, and we all have different personalities, but we will always be there to help out. When the chips are down, get the dip out!

It's a standard joke with people who know me that they do not ask me for directions. I'm just as likely to send you to Winnipeg. This past winter, which was very cold but not much snow, was a good driving season. The call came over the radio one day in the morning shuffle. My partner in crime, Jennifer, was in trouble! She had turned a corner and hit black ice and found herself with both front wheels in the ditch. She was braced up against a tree, and there was no way out without a tow. She radioed dispatch that she had about twenty students on board. Nobody was hurt, but she wasn't going anywhere. I was just about to the school with my students, so I got on the radio and let our dispatch know that I could be at Jennifer's aid in about ten minutes to unload her kids onto my bus. Of course, I didn't exactly know where she was, but I knew she wasn't far off. I was the closest to her. Well ... about four drivers were on the air offering to assist her. They gently (right!) suggested that maybe they should help her out, seeing as they knew where she was. I assured them that I was right around the corner from her and that it just made sense for me to go. I could just about hear them holding their breath. Would they have to send the rescue crew out for me too? I just can't live this reputation down! I communicated with Jennifer, who explained how to get to her from the school.

I drove right over to her like I knew what I was doing. I was so relieved when I saw her bus. We had to do a rear door evacuation of the students, as we couldn't open the front door because of the tree. I loaded up all the students and drove us back to the school. The boys got to Jennifer with the tow truck, and all was well. I felt vindicated a little bit. A few drivers shouted out "Good job, 22." At the end of the day, when all is said and done and my bus is parked for the night, I make my way home. As I pull into my garage, I always thank God for once again bringing me home safely. I may get lost, I may wander off the path and land in the ditch, but God is always on my side of the road. He carries me through each and every time. Keep the rubber side down.

CHAPTER TEN

HOW DID I GET HERE?

Jeremiah 29:11 reads, "For I know the plans I have for you … plans to prosper you and not to harm you, plans to give you hope and a future."

Tom T. Hall sang, "I've been everywhere, man."

If I had a song, it would be, "I've worked everywhere, man."

I've worked since I was fifteen. I dropped out of school halfway through grade ten. I just didn't want to be there. My first job was as a waitress. My very first customer ordered two eggs over easy with bacon, white toast, and coffee. I brought the order to the cook at the back, and a few minutes later the bell rang for me to pick up the order. I got to the back where two orders of bacon and eggs were waiting. I took one order and was leaving when the cook told me to take both. I told him I only needed one. He pointed out that I had written "two" on the order form. I said, "Yeah, the guy wants two eggs!" Arrrrgh! How was I supposed to know he would read it as two separate orders? This was the beginning of my working career. I've been working ever since, but not as a waitress, mind you. I've been a barista, a baker's helper, a telemarketer. Some jobs have lasted three years, others three months.

Mom raised us kids to work. There are no free rides anywhere. She worked outside the home; she had to. I learned from an early age about work ethics. I'm amazed at people who have been at the same job for thirty years. Wow! I, on the other hand, have probably held thirty odd jobs throughout my life. It's not that I like change, but I like variety. I can't picture myself doing the same thing over and over and over again for thirty to forty years. Kudos to those who can. Though I've worked at many different jobs, I've always worked. I never specialized at anything in particular, but I've always paid my way.

When my daughter was born, I was unemployed for her first year and a half. I then put her in daycare and resumed working. I ran the gamut of many different undertakings. I cleaned toilets and pumped gas. I worked at the City of Calgary print shop: I was assistant manager of a gas station in Calgary. I've always been fortunate in my job searches. As unqualified as I am, I would usually get a decent job.

I went to Southern Alberta Institute of Technology many years ago for a program offered to woman only. It was the COTT program: Career Orientation to Trades. In the span of a year, I learned many "male oriented trades" The government was trying to get women involved in trades that are basically male-centred. It was an awesome program and the first pilot of its kind. I took auto mechanics, welding, carpentry, sheet metal, baking, and power engineering. This last one was a yearlong course that was condensed to six months. We had the option of writing the government exam afterwards. I passed and earned a Power Engineering B ticket. I worked in downtown Calgary as a building operator. I stayed with it for about a year and then realized it just wasn't what I wanted.

I also worked for the City of Calgary in the print shop as a bindery operator. It was a good gig back in 1982. The money was good. I was hired at the tail end of the boom. I didn't even need a grade twelve diploma at that time. No qualifications. I was there till 1985. If I had stuck it out, I could be retired now with a great pension. I was twenty-five at the time and not thinking of long term. I was bored with the job. So many people asked how I could quit such a good job.

My mother asked me once if I measured my esteem by the job I had or the way I made a living. I right away said no. But, if I'm being honest, I did. What I did for a living was a measurement of who I was. I see that as being so shallow now. It was a pat on the back when I told people, "I work for the City of Calgary." It was a status thing. When I told you I was assistant manager of a gas station, I felt like I was important. On the other hand, when I shared that I cleaned toilets for a living, I wouldn't exactly crow about it. When I received my Power Engineering ticket, I really thought I was all that and a bag of chips! Look at me. Really, all this entitled me to was being able to operate a boiler at no higher than 250 psi. In other words, I could manage an apartment complex. Yet when I was just a gas pumper, I didn't think much of my job.

I worked for Canada Post for ten years but left because it was such a toxic place to work. Time and again people would ask me how I could leave such a good job. At that time, I was an R.S.M.C. We had just been brought into the union and didn't have the same benefits as others. I like to say I put in my time and got out on good behaviour. To be totally honest, had it not been for my wonderful husband, Jim, I wouldn't have quit. I was so miserable in this job toward the end that it became a hardship to go in every day. The stress of the place was wearing on me. I had the full support of my husband to give my notice. Had I been single, I wouldn't have been able to afford to quit.

I missed the consistency and the schedule that was my life for ten years. For so long I knew what I was going to do each and every day. The words of my mother came back to me. Did I really measure myself by the job I held? It was an ego thing to spout "I work for Canada Post." Where was my identity now? I was forty-nine years old—too young to retire, too old to start a whole new career. I knew I had to work for my own sanity. I'm not one to just sit at home and wait for hubby to come home from work. There's only so much house cleaning I can do, and I don't clip coupons. It took a couple of weeks to adjust and accept the fact that I was no longer a government employee.

The question we ask our children—"What do you want to be when you grow up?"—kept coming back to me. I wasn't afraid of working, and I certainly wasn't lazy. I just didn't know what I was going to do. I worked for a year as a baker's helper in a wonderful little bakery in Black Diamond, Alberta. It was a learning experience, one that would be helpful down the road. From there I went to a local grocery store and worked for another year or so in the A la Carte and Deli section. I knew it wasn't going to be a long-term career ender.

Around this time, a new facility was about to open in our town. It was a long-term care centre with a dementia wing. They were looking to hire for all departments: kitchen, cleaning, clerical, assistants to aids, and bakers. I applied for a baking position, assuring them I was not papered but would be willing to learn. I was hired. I did the baking for all our clients, a total of 150 when at full capacity. I was working in an awesome state of the art kitchen with the best equipment that could be had. I managed quite well, learning as I went, and enjoying it. In a setting like that, there are many regulations and criteria to follow. You deal with many different diets, which you must follow to a T. You have diabetics to bake for, allergies to be mindful of, and hygiene and safety to think about. As I said earlier, I've always managed to come across—or as Mom would say, luck into—a good job. I had no qualifications for this job. I had worked as a baker's helper and had a bit of experience but certainly no schooling.

My working career as Jill of all trades and mistress of none has spanned forty years, give or take a couple. Like I said earlier, my hat is off to those who can work at the same job their whole working life. I just can't. Every report card I ever brought home from school always had the same notation: "If Brenda just applied herself, she could do so much better." It's not that I didn't apply myself, but I was so easily bored! Another of my mother's favourite sayings about me was that I either really liked it or I absolutely hated it. There was never any middle ground with me. She was so right. That still stands true for me. I either like it or I don't. I don't know if that's good or bad. It's just who I am.

If I'd had a different view of school, or had opportunities, could I have done things differently? I consider myself an intelligent person. If I'd had the wherewithal, I could have focused on a different path. Maybe I would have graduated and gone on to university. Maybe I could have been a doctor or lawyer or somebody with initials at the end of my name. But that was never important to me—not enough to pursue it.

I come from a working-class family. We always had food on our table, but we didn't have much left over at the end of the month for splurging. My parents worked very hard to cover the bills and raise three kids. We would be considered poor-folk back then. We used to get bags of clothing from the local Salvation Army store to make rags for the sign shop my parents owned. We would strip buttons and zippers from the clothing and cut the cloth into good sized rags. It was like Christmas when rag bags came in. We got to go through the clothing to see if anything fit us before we took the scissors to it. We loved it! We found some great outfits in there. We didn't think it was odd. That's just the way things were. My folks didn't have extra money to throw around, so we didn't get whole new outfits for the start of school. We were made to appreciate what we had. We were taught that you had to make your way in life. You don't just get a free pass. Pull your fair share wherever you are.

We were all made to go to school, but I really don't think that education was a top priority in my family. We came from working folk, from many generations. Chances are we would all be labourers and not scholars. My sister is the only one who graduated high school. My brother dropped out in grade nine, opting to do a work program at my parents' shop. School was not easy for Danny, and we now realize that he was dyslectic growing up. Back in the sixties, there was no term for that. The system put it down to him being slow because he couldn't read. He became very discouraged and embarrassed about this, and school became an anvil around his neck. He eventually joined the Navy and became a chef, earning his credentials as an intern provincial Red Seal. He was a fabulous cook. He had to work so hard for this. He had to pass the government exams with his learning challenge. He persevered! He did it! From the little boy sitting at the kitchen table with our mother, trying to make sense of the letters that seem backward to him, to a fully qualified chef. What an accomplishment.

IF YOU THINK YOU ARE TOO SMALL TO MAKE A DIFFERENCE, YOU OBVIOUSLY HAVE NEVER SPENT THE NIGHT ALONE WITH A MOSQUITO IN THE ROOM!

Every single one of us has a purpose and a place in this world, whether you're a doctor, a lawyer, a cabinet maker, a waitress, a chambermaid, or a circuit court judge. We're contributing members of society. We cannot live one without the other. We're all as important as the next person, whether we have initials behind our names or crayon markings on our walls. WE ALL MATTER.

My first thought as a child was "What is my purpose? Why am I here?" I was constantly searching for the answer to this question. This quest for knowledge would take me to many different paths on my journey to where I am today. Some days I feel like I've lived enough for four people. I've packed so much into my fifty-eight years. When I look at it, I'm amazed that I'm only fifty-eight.

Psalm 139 is probably one of my favourites of all the Psalms. I certainly can't lay claim to knowing them all, but this verse 16 is very powerful. It reads: "Your eyes saw my unformed body; all the days ordained for me were written in your book before one of them came to be."

Wow! What a statement. God knew the exact plan of my whole life. He has the plan. I've always had an inclination, a belief of some sort, in a divine being. Being raised Catholic gave me some sort of insight. Grandma Eva used to call me her little "Doubting Thomas." She would talk to me at length about Jesus and the

Holy Spirit. I just couldn't see it. I really wanted to, but I needed to see the burning bush, I guess. I prayed to something; I really was scared not too in case there was something there. I just had a hard time believing in something I couldn't touch with my hands or see with my eyes. Ahhhh! That's where faith comes in. I love the mustard seed parable in Matthew 17:20b: "if you have faith as small as a mustard seed, you can say to this mountain, 'Move from here to there,' and it will move. Nothing will be impossible for you."

For many years, through many different relationships and jobs, I was just existing in this life. I had no set course; I was gliding along the pathway, surviving as best I could. I had no guiding force in my sights. I was aimless and lonely. I was spiraling into a world of drinking and drugs. This way of living was at the forefront of my being. My mother was becoming quite concerned about my behaviour. My daughter was nine at the time. I really didn't see a problem. I was working every day; I was paying the bills (more or less), and my child was fed and clothed. But the signs were obviously there.

I should mention here that I come from generations of alcoholics. My grandmother on my mother's side was an alcoholic. She was twelve years sober when she died. I am the daughter of alcoholics; both my mother and natural father were problem drinkers. My stepfather, who was in my life from the age of seven, was a nasty, violent drunk. He has been sober, for forty years now. My mother died three years ago, and as far as I know, she was sober. So, I had plenty of examples to grow by. The age-old question asks if alcoholism is learned behaviour or genetic. I had both sides of that equation. I firmly believe that if I had been tested as a child, I would have been diagnosed as having an addictive personality. I was just waiting to find the substance that would become my downfall.

This is how I know that God was looking out for me even in my darkest hours. I never ventured near the harder core drugs. Something always kept me away from them, scared me from trying them. The drugs I did do were bad enough. The road I was going down was not a pretty one. Suffice to say, through intervention from my family, along with my family doctor, I was admitted to a treatment centre. Through the grace of God, who brought me to the program of Alcoholics Anonymous, I have remained clean and sober for 30 years this August.

The program, the meetings, and the fellowship of the members kept me sober. I found an understanding of God in these rooms. I started to find a faith that I hadn't had since I was a very little child. I started putting my life into this unseen power that I was praying to. I believe in my heart that God led me to A.A. to eventually come back to him. The program of A.A. saved my life, and millions of other lives.

I entered the program in 1991. I worked hard for my sobriety. I was determined to do well for my daughter and for myself. I had to let go of a lot of people in my life when I sobered up, one of whom was my husband at that time. We'd been together for twelve years. I was a year sober when I left him. I couldn't be with him while he was still drinking.

As I look back now, I see that God was with me every step of the way. He never abandoned me. He was always my refuge, even when I didn't see it.

A few years into my sobriety, my sister, who lived in Guelph, gave her life to Christ. She was a passionate Christian, to the point where it was very annoying! I would remind her how she hated it when Grandma would tout her religion to us. I told her I'd had enough spiritual awareness in A.A. The grace of God was keeping me sober. I found that grace in the rooms of A.A. We differed in our opinions, and at times we were pretty heated about it. I didn't want her shoving her views on me! I attended A.A. regularly for twenty years. I got involved in the groups I belonged to and went to different gatherings and many events that celebrated sobriety. When I received my twenty-year medallion, I started backing off meetings. I just wasn't getting out of it what I used to. I was looking for something more. I was feeling restless, and I wanted a deeper relationship with and better understanding of God. I felt that I had gone as far as I could with the program. I owed my life to A.A. I really believe in my heart that had I not gone to treatment, I would be dead or in jail. These are the options to addicts. To alcoholics. I've been to many funerals over the years of friends who just couldn't get it. My brother died when I was three years sober. He was thirty-two years old. His death was a result of alcoholism. I had to bury this boy. He left behind a pregnant wife and two boys aged two and four. His daughter would never know him. This is alcoholism at its finest. It is a deadly disease.

In 2001, I was living in Black Diamond, Alberta and working for Canada Post out of Okotoks. It was a short commute, and I was enjoying living there. I was remarried to someone I had met in the program. Life was good, and we were both involved in A.A. I was introduced to the world of motorcycles through him. We belonged to a group of sober riders. I was ten years sober at this time and still very involved in the program.

Through the program, like any social gathering, I met a lot of people. Some have been long-lasting friendships, and some are members I would see at roundups once or twice a year. When I lived in Black Diamond, I met a lady in the program with whom I connected right away. We were friends for a few years. God puts people in my path sometimes for quite a few years and sometimes for just a little while. Every one of them comes for a reason. I don't always see the reason behind it, and I might even question it, but when I look at it now, it's exactly what I needed at the time. It was through this lady that I would meet a woman who would have a huge impact on my life. Of course, if you had told me then how my life would change so drastically, I would have said you were way off the mark. God's timing is perfect. He knows precisely when to do things. He knew I was ready … or getting ready. He was putting the pieces into play.

"All the days ordained for me were written in your book."

I still get amazed when I think of how the Almighty has it all figured out. How much he loves me. Wow!

CHAPTER ELEVEN

AND SO THE JOURNEY STARTS

Growing up, I didn't have many friends at all. My childhood home was not a place I wanted to bring anyone to. We were a house of secrets. Our family motto was, "What goes on in this house, stays in this house!" I found it hard to build relationships when I was constantly aware of not being able to discuss my family life. I became very good at lying and very good at being alone. This was my norm.

I met Arlene while I was living in Black Diamond through a friend of mine who owned a pet grooming salon. I was there having coffee with her when Arlene walked in. These two knew each other well, so we formed a kind of sort of relationship. We travelled in the same circles, but we weren't that close—just passing acquaintances, you could say. This was what I knew of Arlene: She was a single mother of a ten-year-old girl. She worked three jobs to keep the mortgage payments up and to feed her daughter. She cleaned houses, catered events, and was a school bus driver. She really wasn't the type of person I usually hung out with, but we saw each other sporadically when our mutual friends were together. I really didn't know her well or have an impression of her either way. I saw her as a hard-working woman, pleasant enough, but that was pretty much it. Through our mutual friend, we got to know each other a bit better. Over the years, our mutual friend used us both poorly. Arlene and I would get together to discuss what we could do about the situation. We both agreed that, for our own sakes, we had to let go of this friend. It was not a healthy relationship for any of us. From that point, Arlene and I started to build a closer relationship and stronger bond between us.

When I entered the workforce and the grown-up world, I still didn't have very good skills when it came to socializing. I was a chameleon, always adapting to what you needed. I thought that was the way to make and keep friends. That is such a lonely road to travel. When I joined A.A., I met quite a few people. I did form some very good friendships over the years, and I believe it was in the rooms of A.A. that I grew up. I learned how to look after myself and realized that I don't need to turn myself inside out to get your approval. I'm every bit as important as you. Nobody is above me or beneath me. There was always a stigma attached to my upbringing because of our meager means. I was made to feel like a burden and a black mark because we didn't have the money that my school peers did. I felt humiliated and embarrassed about my family. Compounded with this was the fact that my stepfather was a drunk, and I'm sure the whole town knew.

When I see the kids on my bus, the little groups they form, the camaraderie, I get envious. I don't ever recall that. My heart also goes out to the few who are alone. I see them being alienated from the other kids, how they isolate themselves. I try my best to interact with them, and I pray for them.

During the third week of February, one day is set aside for anti-bullying. The schools make a big to-do about this. Everybody wears pink T-shirts proclaiming kindness to all, equality for all. One day is all this merits. I was the object of bullying in the form of horrible teasing and cruelty from my school mates. It was devastating! Looking back now, I know I often thought of suicide. I was in grades four and up when I would wonder what it would be like to just not wake up. I was such a sad, heartbroken little girl. I so wanted somebody to be my friend, but I didn't know how to do that. To be a friend meant that I had to open up to you, to be honest, to allow you into my world. If that were to happen, you would see the insanity that was my life. My mom was not a happy woman; she was busy picking up the pieces left scattered by her drunken husband. My grandma was an active alcoholic, and there was quite a bit of dysfunction of all sorts in my home. So, you see, I had so many secrets I just couldn't tell you. I didn't dare have you as a friend, in case you found out. I was so worried you would judge me. I judged myself very harshly. God was obviously punishing me for some reason. Why else would this be happening? I was primed to find an escape. This came in the form of drugs, alcohol, and shady "friends."

When Arlene came into my life, I'd been sober ten years. I had grown quite a bit in my identity. I was comfortable in my own skin. After knowing her for about five or six years, she started attending church. She never pushed her ideals or beliefs on me. She knew where I stood on religion. I didn't want a sermon or lecture. I had an understanding of God through the rooms of A.A. She respected this and never crossed the line. But I started seeing a change in this woman over the years. There was a calming presence about her, whereas at one time there had been such a restless and insecure spirit. I could feel a serenity coming from her now.

I started asking her a little at a time about her church. She would talk to me about her changing feelings about Christ. She was a believer now. She had a quiet manner about her that attracted me. In the A.A. program there is a slogan that says, "attraction over promotion." Her quiet persona spoke volumes to me. She wasn't a Bible thumper screaming from the rooftops about her Christianity. She was LIVING it. She was WALKING it. Another of my mother's mantras was, "Show me, don't tell me!" I observed the change and way of Arlene. For the first time in a very long time, I felt a pull.

By this time in her life, Arlene had been quite involved with the church she belonged to and still belongs to. She had been on three or four mission trips to Nicaragua. She would fundraise every year, save bottles, and work markets to achieve her goal. She would come back from two weeks in Nicaragua reinvigorated, reenergized, and focused on Christ. She was pumped, and you couldn't help but feel this power emanating from her. I wanted what she had. She came to see me after her latest trip and brought with her a photo album and many stories. She was already talking about next year's trip. This was June when she came to share with me. We sat at my kitchen table, and I asked her many questions about her trip. Then I asked what the requirements were for going on a mission trip like this.

When I was in grade five, my religious studies teacher, Madame Bussiere, was my favourite teacher. She taught us about the poverty and horrible living conditions in Africa. She told us about missionaries going there to help these people by teaching them to cultivate and grow potatoes. They would also bring the Word of Christ to them. I was hooked. I ran home and told my mother that I wanted to go to Africa to help the poor people plant potatoes. I know that how we interpret things can seem totally different from what might actually have transpired, but to my ten-year-old mind, and to this day, what I heard from my mother when I announced this was, "What makes you think they need you there?"

I remember feeling so dejected, so little and insignificant. Who was I to think I could possibly be needed anywhere or by anyone? I never brought it up again. My mother's comment might have been totally innocent. She was probably distracted, taking care of dinner, trying to figure out how to pay the bills, worrying about her husband, and here I come telling her I want to go to Africa! She just flippantly answered without thinking that this would crush me. It did. For decades, I measured myself by this answer. "What makes you think you're good enough?" This would become my mantra. The saddest thing about it is that I never told her. She died not knowing how her response had affected me. I never shared with her my trips to Nicaragua.

Proverbs 18:21a reads: "The tongue has the power of life and death." I really believe in my heart that my mother didn't mean to be hurtful or cruel. I really think she had no idea how her comment would affect me. It's amazing how such an innocent comment could alter a person's whole view on life. The tongue can cut; it has the power to wound deeply, and it can shatter you. When the person you look to for approval cuts you to the core, even unknowingly, you're left questioning everything. Nothing makes sense anymore. Your whole world is thrown off kilter.

This lesson has served me well as a bus driver. Maybe that's why I had to learn it. I know what it's like to be so enthused about something only to have that dream dashed by a few misspoken words. I try to the best of my ability to listen to the kids on the bus, to hear their dreams and plans, to celebrate with them. I don't want to crush their spirit with inconsiderate ramblings. The nuggets that the kids share with me are of the utmost importance to them at this time. They have chosen to share with me! I am privileged and honoured to be singled out in this matter. To you and me it might be the silly goings-on of a child, but to them it is enormous, it is life changing. It's their very existence and who they are. I thank God that he allows me to be part of this awesome experience. This is a rainbow gift in my day.

Arlene said that the only requirement to go on a mission trip was to be a Christian. I asked her for the definition of a Christian, and she asked if I believed that Jesus died to forgive my sins. Did I believe that he had risen? Well, of course I did! After all, I did go to Catholic school. I was an altar girl; I served mass. Of course, I was a Christian. Wasn't I? There is HUGE difference between being a Christian and being a CHRISTIAN. I was about to find that out.

I told her I wanted to go to on the next trip to Nicaragua. She put me in touch with the powers that be, and I applied with Samaritan's Purse, who was leading the trip. I met monthly with the group of twenty-three teammates that would be part of this trip. I received my husband's blessing, raised the money needed, took time off work, and prepared to go to Bluefields, Nicaragua. It wasn't Africa, it wasn't planting potatoes, but it was close enough! I was on my way.

CHAPTER TWELVE

FINDING JESUS IN BLUEFIELDS, NICARAGUA (NOT THAT HE WAS LOST)

In preparation for my trip, I saved the required fee of $3,100.00. That would cover airfare and two nights at a hotel (one coming and one going). All of our meals were covered, as we would have a cook on premises to prepare all our meals. We would be staying at the lodgings of Pastor Ed and his wife, Ligia. Our out-of-pocket expenses were whatever souvenirs we bought and meals at the airport. Our team consisted of twenty-four people. This included a couple of husband-and-wife teams and a couple of fifteen-year-old boys who came with their parents. Eleven women and fourteen men made up our team. We would be together for twelve days. This trip was the tenth one for our team leader, Marinus. He was very familiar with the terrain and the everyday goings-on of the area. Part of my getting ready for the trip was to get a TWINRIX Hepatitis shot. I also took malaria pills a couple of weeks before we left. I was prepared for the eventuality of anything that we could encounter. I am basically a healthy person, but I didn't want to travel without precautions.

Our team met once a month leading up to our date of travel to go over what we would be doing, where we would be going, and what to expect. About six to eight of us had never been on a mission trip before. It was very comforting to go with a group who knew what was in store and could guide us along the way. We were going into a foreign country, where the language was primarily Spanish. I found that my being French helped out in understanding a bit of their language. During our monthly get togethers, we reviewed what was expected of us, our conduct, and our wish to serve God and his people. I admitted to my teammates from the first meeting that I believed in God, but I wasn't sure that it was with the same fervor and faith that they had. That mattered not to these wonderful people. They accepted me into their fold with open arms.

We were given a list of what we should take with us, and we each had a fifty-pound limit. Along with clothing, toiletries, and the usual holiday fare, I collected little toys and souvenirs to bring to the children we would be meeting. We also brought our own linens for our beds, which we would leave behind for our hosts to use in the future. Most teams that travel and use Pastor Ed's home leave behind clothing, health care items, and anything that can be used by the community, like toothpaste, Aspirin, female products, and so much more. These items are so expensive to buy for the locals. Food is more important than having to worry about shampoo. What we take for granted is mind boggling.

Along with our fifty-pound duffel bag for personal use, we were responsible to tote another fifty-pound duffel bag each with all the supplies we'd be bringing to our mission. These supplies included tools of all kinds, such as hammers, drills, tape measurers, screwdriver sets, electric drills, saws, nails, and screws. Any and all that we could get together for the trip. We gathered all these over the months leading up to our trip.

We also brought duffel bags full of eyeglasses, which came from the Samaritan's Purse head office. We brought equipment to perform eye exams and even a box of one thousand pairs of new sunglasses that were donated. We had donations of new clothing articles to pass around, bags of new baby clothes, and all kinds of baby supplies for the women's shelter we'd be visiting. We were overwhelmed with donations from church members who wanted to bless us with all these gifts. We had twenty-four duffel bags weighing fifty pounds each that were full to the brim with supplies that we would leave in Bluefields. Two days before we were due to fly out, we all met at the church for packing night. We arranged all of our donations and sorted and itemized them into different piles. We then packed them all into the bags, weighed them on a scale, and got them ready to go.

Our mission would be two-fold. For five years, teams had been coming out to Bluefields and were slowly building the Verbo Christian School. It was a two-storey school that would educate from EC to grade twelve. Our team would be erecting a set of concrete stairs that would lead to the second level. Keep in mind that we didn't have modern equipment to do this job. We had an old (ancient) cement mixer that was as ornery as an old donkey on a hot day. It was held together with duct tape and a lot of prayers. We would get the bags of sand and crushed rock and mix it in the machine, hoping it held out. The first few days were spent laying the form and the rebar. It was sweltering hot in the high thirties Celsius.

While construction was going on, another phase of the mission was to provide an eyeglass clinic. This is where I spent most of my trip. I will expand on both of these projects in a little bit.

It was getting close to leaving time! I was getting so excited. I packed and repacked my own bag I don't know how many times. We were told to bring a pair of work gloves with us, as there would be none for us there. I went to hardware section at Walmart the day before we left and found a pair that was sturdy enough to work with. I gawked at the price—$15.00! Geez! Oh well, I needed them. I put them in my bag and zipped it up.

One more sleep to go. I was ready. All was in order at home. This would be the longest I would be away from Jim, but I had his full support about this trip. He had no desire to go, but he respected the fact that this was important to me. I prepared meals for him that I froze, and I left him a list of household needs. I let him know when to feed the dog. I was worse than a parent leaving their child for the first time. He just smiled. He never did eat the prepared meals. I think he lived in restaurants for two weeks, but the dog survived quite well. He did manage to water my two plants … I think the day before I came back. I wasn't going to be in contact with him for two weeks, as I wasn't taking my cell phone. I left a list of phone numbers with him in case of emergency, and he could get through to me at Pastor Ed's house. Some teammates brought their phones and laptops, but I chose to experience the whole trip without gadgets. It was suggested that we focus on our mission and the people we would be helping. It wasn't forbidden to communicate with our family, but a stronger bond was formed when we disconnected and concentrated on why we were there. I told Jim I preferred to immerse myself in the journey. He was fine with that. I emailed him from our hotel the night before we were to return home to let him know our time of arrival. I have never been a big computer whiz. As far as cell phones go, I use it more for emergencies or as a means of contact for my bus parents. It really wasn't a big deal to unplug for two weeks. I didn't miss it or go through withdrawal.

As well as being physically prepared, we were advised to be spiritually prepared for this trip. As a group, we would pray for our health and protection from hardships. We prayed to be united on our quest, to be ready for whatever we faced. The elements alone could be very trying. The heat was unfamiliar to us Canadians. The humidity was a force of its own. We were guided to pursue our motives for this trip. I prayed to the God of my understanding and asked him to guide me where I could be of service, to protect me, and to help me as I ventured out.

Over and above the physical content of our mission, we were on this trip to bring the Word of Jesus to these people. I didn't know what to expect from this. I just figured we would let these poor people know that they were loved. That was that. I was so ignorant, so out of the ball field! I was going to save these poor souls! I'm sure God was chuckling at my chutzpah! In my heart, I wanted to go to Bluefields to help these people and to share with them what I had. To give back where I could. To just love on them. What happened instead was that the tables were turned. I had no warning, no precognition. They gave to me, they shared with me, they loved on me. They didn't even know me. For two wonderful weeks, I cried and sobbed tears of joy, of anguish, of pure love. Unconditional, no strings attached. If I had any expectations about this trip, they were met ten-thousand-fold.

On February 18, 2013, twenty-four of us met at the Calgary International Airport at 5:00 a.m. We were all wearing our mission T-shirts that proclaimed we were on our way to Nicaragua. It was very exciting to be part of this group. We kissed our loved ones goodbye and prepared to load all our gear. This alone was a challenge, as we had our personal bags and the twenty-four bags of supplies we were taking. God's grace saw us all through with no mishaps. We made our way to the departure gate and waited to board our plane. As we waited, our team leader prayed with us for a safe journey, connecting flights, health, and perseverance, as it would be a very long day.

We boarded around 8:00 a.m. and flew to Houston. Here we would have a six-hour layover. Samaritan's Purse had a huge room for us that was furnished with chairs and couches. We all sprawled out. We read and played cards, and some of our teammates practised making balloon animals. They would amaze and entertain the children in Nicaragua with these gifts. We toured around the airport itself. The Houston International is an amazing airport! There is an echo chamber there where you yell out to the ceiling and it yells back. It's incredible. We had lunch at the B.B.Q. restaurant that's there. The best ribs and chicken I've ever had. Quite a few of the team had been there a few times, but to us newbies it was really cool.

We finally boarded our plane about 6:00 p.m. and were now heading for Managua, Nicaragua. Managua is the capital city of Nicaragua. It has a population of 2.2 million people in the city proper and over 2.5 million in the metropolitan area. It's situated between the Pacific Ocean and the Caribbean Sea and nestled between Honduras and Costa Rica. The primary language is Spanish, but you will also encounter German, Italian, English, and French. The main resources of Nicaragua are coffee, bananas, tobacco, and sugarcane.

We arrived in Managua about 9:30 p.m. and lined up to go through customs and get all our luggage and supply bags. This was quite a process, as we had so much to check, and we had to make sure we had everything. Finally, we were ready to head out. We were to stay in Managua overnight. Our hotel was right across the road from the airport, so we walked over with all our bags. That first gulp of Nicaraguan air was breathtaking. It was at least twenty-eight degrees Celsius when we stepped outside of the airport. Humid! Wow, what a contrast from what we'd left back home. It was now about 11:00 p.m., and we grouped up to get our instructions for the morning, particularly where we would all meet for breakfast before continuing our journey to Bluefields. Bed never felt so good!

Morning came, and I took what would be my last hot shower for two weeks before going to breakfast. We had a feast and discussed the next step. We'd all be boarding a bus that would be picking us up in thirty minutes. It would be a six-hour bus trip cross country, where we would then disembark and get onto a boat for another two-and-a-half-hour trip across the Pacific Ocean to our final destination of Bluefields. The reason for this extended trip was that we were carrying so much weight with us—a total of 2,400 pounds. This would be too heavy for the small biplane combined with our individual weights. Coming back at the end of our trip, we wouldn't be bringing the supply bags, so we'd be able to take a small plane right from Bluefields to the airport in Managua.

The whole travelling experience by bus and boat was incredible. The sights and sounds were out of this world: the calls and cries of the local birds as we travelled across the huge azure expanse, the sun reflecting off the sea as we made our way through small villages dotted across the horizon, little thatched homes of the local people who came out to cheer us on and bless us with their smiles. The weather was perfect. I'm so glad to have experienced the whole process.

While we were waiting to load on the boat, we had to stay clear while the Nicaraguan police patrolled all our bags with their drug sniffing dogs. We got the all-clear and boarded what is called panga boats, on account of the noise they make ... *panga, panga, panga*. There were two boats to carry us all.

As we were approaching Bluefields, which is an island with a population of 45,000 people, we could see the little huts along the shoreline. They were little more than shanties. When we pulled up to dock, the locals came out to greet us. They knew we were missionaries and that we were there to help and be with them. The children came running out to see us and love on us. I was overwhelmed at the open-armed love they heaped on us. I was already sobbing! This would happen quite a bit while I was there.

We were here! We were actually here! It was close to 4:00 p.m. It had been a long journey, and we were all pretty tuckered, excited, hungry, and so grateful to be here.

Pastor Ed met us at the dockside, along with a few of his workers. All of our bags and supplies were loaded, and we were bound for our home for the next two weeks. Praise God!

The home we'd be staying in was a big B and B. This house was actually built by Amish people many years ago for Pastor Ed and his wife, Luiga. They host many different mission groups throughout the year. It's a two-storey house with a large living room as you first enter. This leads to a large dining area that holds two very large tables that seated us all. On the main floor there are three large bedrooms with two to three sets of bunk beds in each. There are two bathrooms on this floor. The guys stayed on the lower floor, and the girls were upstairs, where there were four bedrooms, with bunk beds in each. Pastor Ed and his wife had a bedroom of their own up there. There were also two bathrooms up there. All bathrooms had showers, and we were asked to either have a shower in the morning or in the afternoon. Water was a limited commodity, so we couldn't take it for granted like we did at home. I opted to have my showers in the evening. After a full day of working, I was very grateful to get into a cold-water shower.

We all settled into our rooms, made up our beds, put away our personal effects, and made sure that our luggage was zipped up to prevent scorpions from sneaking in. We never did see any on this trip, I would, however, encounter them on my 2015 trip. We had plenty of geckos in our room. They didn't bother us, and they kept the mosquito population down. We had fans in our bedrooms, which we aimed right at ourselves. It was very, very, very hot! I lucked out in that I had a single cot to myself—first dibs. There were two sets of bunk beds in our room and a single cot. I grabbed the cot as soon as we got in, and it was right by the window. I don't do bunk beds anymore. I get up to go to the bathroom too often. Of course, being right by the window gave me an earful of the dogs that patrolled our gated-in grounds, and the roosters who crowed at all hours of the night. I thought they only crowed when the sun came up. NO! They crow anytime they want.

There was a huge wrap-around veranda as you came up the stairs, where rocking chairs were just waiting for you to sit and rest. We spent many evenings there just enjoying the cool breeze and the songs of the local birds. We would recap our day there and talk about tomorrow. We would share the joy and love we'd experienced that day. It was our down time. It was a time to renew and praise God.

When we first arrived at the house, we all set about getting settled. We then met in the dining room for supper, followed by our first meeting. Here we would discuss where we would each be working. There was to be a team heading to the school to have a look at the construction. There was also a team going to the church where the eyeglass clinic would be held. Every night we would come together after supper and decide where everybody would be heading the next day. It was suggested that we try different things on this trip. Don't just stick with what you're comfortable with. Try your hand at the construction and also put in a couple of days at the eye clinic. Do what you can. We also had a few other trips as well as our primary chores. We would spend a day at the women's shelter, a day with the children at a feeding program for them, and a day to ourselves along the beach and the market.

Samaritan's Purse collects used eyeglasses from different organizations throughout the year. The little boxes you see at the ophthalmologist office that says you can drop off your old pairs of glasses here get picked up and brought to the Samaritan's Purse office in Calgary. They are then brought to Spy Hill Jail in Calgary, where the prisoners refurbish and clean them. They are then separated into their prescription categories and sent back to Samaritan's Purse. These are all labeled and sorted to be sent all over the world on different mission trips. Our teammate Michele has been trained by Samaritan's Purse to oversee the eyeglass clinics on the mission trips. This requires a lot of preparation. She must go into the office and sort and prepare all the glasses that will be coming with us. As well, she has to pack all the equipment that will be used for the exams and the tools we will need to adjust and fix the glasses on site. (Sight … get that?) All of this was packed into our supply bags. We needed special permission from the Nicaraguan government to bring these glasses over.

Again, God saw us through all the paperwork. We were blessed to not have any major obstacles to overcome on our journey to

Bluefields. We were of the mindset that we were in a foreign country, so we would be considerate and adhere to all their rules. As missionaries, we weren't the most loved of the Nicaraguan government, as we were there to bring the Word of Jesus to the people. Better to keep the people ignorant and dependant on the government than on Jesus. There is a freedom in knowing Jesus. Many missionaries have been persecuted for trying to teach the gospel to others. We are so fortunate here in Canada that we can pray where we want, when we want, and without punishment. On the other hand, so many of us still don't know about Jesus. So who is better off? The man who knows nothing but seeks to find something? Or the man who knows something and chooses to do nothing? The difference between religion and spirituality is that religion is the man who sits in church thinking about fishing, but spirituality is the man who is fishing and thinking about God! I heard that tidbit in an A.A. meeting.

I like to commune with God wherever I am, whatever I'm doing. To me, church is a coming together of fellow Christians, a sharing and worshipping, a learning of the Bible. But I can also do church in my back yard. I listen to God when I see the birds at my bird feeders in the front yard. I love their individual songs. I worship God when I see the new buds on my trees, and when my new tree we planted two years ago is flowering. I talk to God in my bus when the roads are bad, when I see the sun rising over the mountains, and when my eye catches the deer about to dart in front of me. I praise him when I see a child smile or hear him laugh heartily, when I see a rainbow or a sundog, and when I hear the children singing on the bus. I see God in everything that is good on this earth. When a ladybug lands on my arm, I thank him. I am so grateful to live where I do, to know freedom of choice and religion, to live a good life as a good person. The more I turn to God and rely on him and not me, the more rainbows I see.

CHAPTER THIRTEEN

SCHOOLING SHOULD NOT BE A PRIVILEGE

The first Verbo Christian School was started in 1986. There is now a second school that was built in 2016 adjacent to the church and orphanage. Both schools educate from K-12 and have a combined enrolment of about 1,300 with sixty-three teachers and administrative personnel. Pastor Ed's wife, Ligia, has worked at the school for many years. She fundraises tirelessly and devotes her time and energy to the cause of the children. She believes wholeheartedly that every child should have an education.

We in Canada are so fortunate to have schooling as a given. When my daughter was of school age, I went to the school, registered her, and prepared for her to enter Kindergarten. I had no doubts, no fears, no qualms about her going. I took it for granted as my right and hers that she would go to school. She would be taught and would receive an education. She was entitled to this as a Canadian.

The same can't be said about Nicaragua. In order to go to school, a child must be sponsored. Those fortunate enough to get a sponsor will receive an education. The sponsor pays for tuition and school fees, which will pay the teachers. The sponsorship will provide a hot meal daily at the school, uniforms for the student, and supplies. Some students come from a long way to attend the school. Here they are taught how to read and write, basic skills that will be needed for the workforce. From the age of ten, they are trained in trades such as sewing, carpentry, agriculture, handcrafts, computer skills, and music to better prepare them for sustaining careers. This is only if they have a sponsor. If they don't, the alternative is quite different and quite sad. Seventy-nine per cent of the population live on less than $2.00 US per day. Twenty-seven per cent are undernourished.

The country of Nicaragua was once affluent and booming. Its main exports were fruit and lumber, as well as other commodities. In September 2007, Hurricane Felix wreaked havoc throughout the nation. The incredible poverty that runs through Bluefields is heartbreaking. Nicaragua is the second poorest country in the Western Hemisphere. The devastation of Felix is still felt all over. I did see growth and renewal when I returned to Bluefields in 2016. It was very noticeable, and the economy is slowly, very slowly, turning. The people stand strong, and they will rebuild. They want their children to get an education, to set themselves free from the oppression, to help rebuild their communities. And this is happening.

When I was there on my last trip in 2016, at Pastor Ed's home, I met a young man who came by the house to visit Ed and Ligia. He shared supper with us and told us in rather good English that he had graduated that year from the Verbo Christian School with high honours. He was the first and only recipient from the whole of

Nicaragua to receive a full scholarship to the Cost Rica University. Here he would enter an Engineering and Agricultural program. It would be a two-year degree. The dilemma was his mother. She didn't want her eldest leaving home; he was a bread winner for the family, and his leaving would take away the few coins he brought in. He was torn about this gift that had been handed to him. His mother couldn't see the long-term benefits of him getting an education and returning to his community with skills that would benefit his homeland. She could only see the bread that was needed for today. It was a double-edged sword for this young man.

Pastor Ed counselled the mother, who was a parishioner at his church. She did eventually see that, in the long run, this would be the wisest and most beneficial choice. Pastor would make sure that the family wouldn't go hungry while the boy was away. What an opportunity for this young man. To have worked so hard, to conquer so much, and to be able through the grace of God to return home and help his family on a long-term basis. To be able to break a cycle of illiteracy and poverty, all because this boy was sponsored by someone, somewhere in the world. This precious gift of education we take for granted and throw away because we don't want to go to school. We'd rather work at a menial job than get an education. It's such a bother! It's so boring! Who cares about reading and writing? I hate homework.

The alternative in Nicaragua, if the children don't have a sponsor, is not very pretty. Children are set to work at a very young age. It is their birthright. What is allowed in Nicaragua would be considered child labour in Canada. There are no social services or unemployment insurance benefits, no Salvation Armies to turn to, no shelters for the homeless. No soup kitchens. Bluefields has the highest rate of teen pregnancy and AIDS per capita of anywhere in Nicaragua.

Pastor Ed took us to the rock quarry one day after our workday at the school. This huge rock quarry is where many people were employed. Whole families worked there. Children as young as five were working side by side with their parents and siblings. Their days began as the sun rose and went till the sun set. In the stifling heat, these people would sit all day, hammer in hand, and smash rocks into smaller rock. They would then transfer these into fifty-pound burlap bags. These bags were what we used with sand to make cement. Each bag brought them eighty-five cents. They might fill two or three bags a day. This is the alternative when you're not sponsored to go to school.

Another means of employment, which has thankfully been outlawed, was to work at the landfill. People would go to the landfill and rake through it to see if there was anything worth salvaging. They would go through the refuse barefoot, among rats and vultures (we saw them), to find anything of value that could be sold or used. The government finally shut this down, as there were quite a few deaths. The landfill would be set on fire to allow for space, and people were getting horribly burned and even killed trying to rescue some piece of garbage. The government set up a recycling centre, which we toured, and here the people were paid to sort through and separate all materials. Slowly, there is a turning and a much-needed change of attitude concerning poverty and all it entails. The people of Nicaragua want to get out of this rut and better themselves. This has to start with the children, with education.

The funds required for this trip are allocated to different areas: our plane tickets, our two nights' hotel room, the board we pay to Pastor Ed and to the cook who is hired locally to feed us for two weeks, all the food we need, and the two housekeepers who are also hired locally. There are benefits for the community when a mission team comes over. We provide a small income for a few people. As well, most team members tip the cook and cleaners before we head back home. Another wage is paid to local labourers who help us out at the construction site. They're awesome workers, so pleased and grateful for the work. They are all Christians hired through Pastor Ed's church. One thousand dollars per team member is transferred to a Nicaragua bank in trust of Pastor Ed and Samaritan's Purse. These funds are usually deposited a couple of months before the trip. This allows materials to be purchased for the construction site, which need to be brought in via boat from Managua. Very expensive. We bring bags of tools with us to leave behind as gifts, as it's so pricey for them to buy anything extra.

When we arrive, everything is waiting and ready for us to begin. There is so much preparation and organizing that goes into a mission trip. Anything can happen. Delays occur, shipments don't come in on time, weather can play a factor, illness among the team can happen. We had a few of our members down very sick for a few days. We had to actually quarantine them, but all ended well. Praise God again.

We're very diligent about our expenses and our balance in our mission bank account. One family was in desperate need of medical attention for a young child. Pastor Ed was summoned to their home. He assessed the situation and met with us to discuss the issue. These people had little enough food, and they certainly couldn't afford to go to a doctor and possibly buy medication. We all gladly passed the hat around for Pastor to bring to the family. We were able to assist like this in different scenarios with the guidance of Pastor Ed. He knows his flock and who is in need. He was the first to warn us about some people who, unfortunately, target missionaries. We were to bring any requests from people to him, and he would let us know if it was legit or not. It's so easy to want to give to all the needy there, but Ed advised us that this wouldn't help and was only a Band-aid solution. Throwing money at them was just showing them how to keep asking for money instead of teaching them how to earn it. The old "teach a man to fish" lesson. Pastor Ed is such a wise, gentle, loving man. He and his wife do such awesome work in their community. They are true angels sent by God.

From our bank account, we were able to earmark $200.00 in US funds. With this, we bought and packaged seventy-two food bags to distribute to the community. Pastor Ed chose the families that would benefit from it. It's unfortunate that we couldn't provide for all, but we were grateful that we could help a few. These food bags consisted of rice, beans, sugar, flour, coffee, toothpaste and toothbrushes, hygiene products for women, deodorant, toilet paper, and soap. I was very humbled as I helped prepare these bags. We prayed as we placed items into bags, and we praised God for all he was doing.

I wanted to do so much more; I felt this just wasn't enough. There was so much need and not enough people helping. I brought this up at our nightly get togethers and shared how I felt so inadequate and insignificant. I was feeling suffocated by the never-ending need. It was almost a panic that I couldn't do enough. My team prayed with me and assured me that what I was feeling, this empathy and compassion, was all a part of this experience called love. But why does it have to hurt so much? I want to fix the whole world. I was told that I was helping one person at a time. Who knew what this person would do with that help? Maybe through me, through them, they would help ten people, and those ten people might help one thousand more. It all has to start with just one person.

We spent a day in the truck delivering the food packages. Along with the food, a Spanish Bible was also provided to each family. When we'd arrive at the home, four or five of our team would go with Ed to bring the gift. The homes are very small, usually housing six or more people. One room usually makes up the entire abode. The families would greet us so warmly. Ed would interpret for us, and we also had a couple on our team who spoke Spanish. We were treated like royalty and asked to come in and chat for a few minutes. They would be impeccably dressed in mended but very clean clothing. Their dirt floors were swept clean, and whatever they had they would offer to us. We'd always ask if we could pray with them and if they had any requests for prayer. During these visits, I would just stand and listen. Some members would take turns praying, praising, and worshipping. I don't want to say I was uncomfortable, but I wasn't really sure what to do, so I just observed. I was never made to feel that I had to jump in and pray out loud. I was very content to just take it all in and see the joy on the faces of these people as they expressed how grateful they were to God for sending us here. We were their angels sent right from the Almighty. I kept thinking, *But we haven't done much.*

In Mark 12:41–44, Jesus tells the story of the widow's offering.

> Jesus sat down opposite the place where the offerings were put and watched the crowd putting their money into the temple treasury. Many rich people threw in large amounts. But a poor widow came and put in two very small copper coins, worth only a few cents. Calling his disciples to him, Jesus said, "Truly I tell you; this poor widow has put more into the treasury than all the others. They all gave out of their wealth; but she, out of her poverty, put in everything - all she had to live on."

Giving from the heart is worth so much more than gold or silver. It's a feeling that you just can't put a monetary value on. Once you do it, you want to keep on doing it. I do, anyway. It's a hot water bottle for your heart. Try it ... you won't be disappointed. I found out in Nicaragua, among many things, that it's the simplest gestures that make the biggest difference. It's the sharing and caring and the loving on people, the praying and the crying with, the joy and the compassion you open your heart to.

∞

A few days prior to September school start up, teachers and bus drivers from our district get together for a rah-rah day. We have guest speakers come and share motivational stories; we get pumped up for the return of another year. We also cry a few tears! Summer is over. A couple of years ago, I received a starfish pin attached to a little card. This card explained the meaning behind the starfish. This was adapted from Loren Eiseley's work. I still cherish my starfish.

The Starfish Story by Loren Eiseley:

One day a man was walking along the beach when he noticed a boy picking up and gently throwing things into the ocean.

Approaching the boy, he asked, "Young man, what are you doing?"

The boy replied, "Throwing starfish back into the ocean. The surf is up, and the tide is going out. If I don't throw them back, they'll die.

The man laughed to himself and said, "Do you realize there are miles and miles of beach and hundreds of starfish? You can't make any difference."

After listening politely, the boy bent down, picked up another starfish, and threw it into the surf. Then smiling at the man, he said, "I made a difference to that one."

That's life in a nutshell, isn't it? If I can make a difference to one student on my bus, it will all be worth it. I think for me the key is to try. Just try. Don't think you can't, or assume someone will look after it, or that you simply don't know where to start. Just try.

∞

Pastor Ed picked us up at the construction site one day to bring us back to the house. This was one of the days I was helping with the mixing of the cement and hauling fifty-pound buckets of wet cement to the boys, who would pour it down into the forms. It was great physical work—dirty, but so invigorating! Had I been at the eyeglass clinic that day, I would have missed the side trip we took on our way home. We climbed into the truck. I always sat shotgun with Pastor Ed. The A.C. was blasting up front. Some team members clambered into the back of the truck and packed in as many as we could. There really are no road and vehicle bylaws in Bluefields. I once saw a family of six (seriously) riding on a moped!

Pastor Ed detoured to the rock quarry. We had visited it only briefly a couple days earlier. He pulled up, shut the truck off, and told us all to get out. People were working away in the quarry, whole families working side by side. The youngest with their little hammers doing what they could. Older people sitting in the full sun—no hats, no footwear, no sunscreen—smashing rock. Pastor Ed gathered us around him and started pulling out a dozen food bags from the back of the truck. These were set aside from the other food bags that had been brought. Ed had specific families in mind to hand these to.

We paired up in groups of three and four and went to where Pastor Ed pointed us to. I went with two teammates, Aaron and Melissa, and we headed to a single woman who was sitting cross-legged, head down, and hammering on her pile of rocks in front of her. Her name was Isabella. Walking toward her, I ventured to guess she was in her fifties … maybe younger or older, it's hard to tell, as the sun can do so much damage to the skin. We were told her name was Isabella. An interpreter followed us, and as we approached her, she unfolded herself. She seemed pretty stiff as she greeted us. She was very shy, and it was explained to her through interpretation that we wanted to bless her with this food. We would also like to pray with her if she would allow it. She agreed, and we held hands and prayed with her. Again, I just allowed the feeling to come over me. I felt the love and peace of the moment.

When we were done, I reached for her hands to hold, and I felt how callused and rough they were. The other team members were walking away, so it was just her and I standing there. I looked into this woman's eyes; I just wanted to convey to her how I wanted to help her, how I would like nothing better than to lighten her load. I could only look into her eyes and hope she understood. I brought her hands to my lips and kissed them. I was crying by the time I let her go. She placed the food bag behind her and set herself back down onto the hard ground. She smiled at me and continued working. I walked back to the truck and asked Pastor Ed if her food would be safe. Not everybody received a food bag, I was worried that being by herself, somebody might try to take it. Ed assured me she would be looked after.

I stood looking at that woman, thinking that only through the grace of God it wasn't me. The only difference between me and her was geography. I was born in Canada; she was born here. She had a faith that shone through. I wanted to do something. As we were getting ready to leave, I ran back to Ed and asked if I could leave something with her. Ed said sure. I yanked the passenger door open, reached into my bag, and retrieved the work gloves I had complained about paying $15.00 for. They were still almost new. I looked up to the heavens and sent a silent plea to the God of my understanding. I just wanted to show this woman that I cared.

As I walked back toward her, she started getting up, and I motioned her to stay seated. It was just her and I. We didn't need to speak. I reached over and handed her the gloves. I was crying then and also as I'm writing this. She took them in her hands and smiled at me and then nodded and said "Gracias." There was age in those eyes, and wisdom and weariness. I felt so humbled in her presence.

I turned away and started walking back to the truck. I glanced over my shoulder and saw that she was using the gloves like a fan to cool her face off. I got into the truck, sobbing, just so overcome with emotion. I was a basket case. Pastor Ed got in and started the truck. Everybody was loaded, so we pulled away. I took one last look at Isabella. Her head was down, bent over her work, wearing the gloves! She made the difference in me. She was the reason that the next morning, February 25, 2013, at 6:41 a.m., I gave my life to Christ, right there in the kitchen archway with Pastor Ed and Arlene to bear witness. If this woman could have such a faith and love for Jesus, even in her circumstances, who was I not to believe? This was a turning point for me. It took going to Bluefields, Nicaragua to see and feel the love of God. I didn't plant a potato, but the seed of love was planted in me. Isabella had no idea what she did for me that day. I asked Pastor Ed in 2016 when I returned for a final trip if he knew where she was. He knew who I was referring to but didn't know where she was. She could have moved, or maybe even died. I know she was my starfish, and for that I am so grateful.

CHAPTER FOURTEEN

SEEING IS BELIEVING

I'm sure most people have gone for an eye exam. Quite of few of my students wear glasses. Young kids even wear contacts. I tried wearing contacts once, but it was not a good experience. My eye guy at the local Walmart helped me put them in and then told me to walk around the store for half an hour to get used to them. They felt good. I returned to the store, and he told me to take them out, which I couldn't. Every time I tried to remove them I would close my eyes tight. This went on for quite a while. Finally, he told me to go home and try to remove them later. I went home, and as I was having lunch, I reached up and removed one and then the other. I then walked over to the garbage can and promptly deposited them. I phoned my guy and told him I would carry on wearing glasses. I was not prepared to poke myself in the eye on a daily basis.

We bring our children in for eye exams at an early age. We're fortunate that we can just call the office and set up an appointment to get our eyes checked. A lot of benefit plans pay for this, and seniors are entitled to free exams. The whole process is painless and very thorough. Nowadays with the state-of-the art equipment, your eyes can be checked every which way—front, back, sideways. Diseases can be detected, such as glaucoma and even cancer. It's not just eye charts anymore! It's quite involved.

Our Nicaraguan team was to provide an eyeglass clinic on our trip to Bluefields. The last time an eyeglass clinic had been there was about five years previously. Whoever wanted to have their eyes examined and receive glasses had to sign up. We held the clinic at the church, where we would be set up by 8:00 a.m., and we'd work till about 5:00 p.m. We took a break for lunch, which was brought out to us from Pastor Ed's house.

Michelle, our teammate, was trained in eyeglass clinics, and she gave us a quick run-through of how things would work. This was going to be a very primitive eye exam for these people, but it accomplished what we needed to outfit them. The worst part about the heat and sun of Nicaragua is the damage it can do to the naked eye. You're so close to the equator, and the sun is so fierce. Most people have no protection from it. So many people, young and old, have a sort of film over their eyes. This wasn't glaucoma but a disease caused by the direct sun. Without protection, it would just progress to where it would eventually lead to blindness. There was an operation, or medical treatment, to fix it, but this cost money.

We were given one thousand pairs of sunglasses before we left, and we made sure that everybody we saw at the clinic received a pair. We were especially concerned about the small children.

Our eye exam included an eye chart. Keep in mind that most locals were illiterate. Our chart didn't have the letters of the alphabet but the letter E transposed in different ways. We would point to the letter and they would tell us which way the letter was pointing: left, right, upside down, or right side up. This worked! I had my doubts at first, but what did I know? We were able to communicate with them and determine from the graph where they were vision-wise. As I said, it was very primitive, but it was instrumental in helping them.

We had also brought six hundred pairs of glasses with us from the Samaritan's Purse office. We had all different prescriptions, as well as bifocal, progressive, and clear glass. There were different sizes for adults and youth. These were all sorted by prescription and strength.

We would check the client from the list and have them come sit in front of the chart. We would point with a ruler down the line and ask which way the E was facing. When they got to the point where they could no longer tell, we'd check the line, assess their vision, and find a pair of glasses for them. We would then have them try the pair on and check the chart again. The difference was phenomenal! They could see. The joy on their faces said it all. I didn't need to understand their language to know that this was working. Once they had their glasses, they were led to another station, where another teammate would make sure the glasses fit properly. They would also get a pair of sunglasses. From this station, they were asked if they wanted somebody to pray with them. They would be escorted to a station where two of our team members were sitting and would pray with them for a few minutes.

I helped at the eyeglass clinic for about eight of my days on the trip. It was such a gratifying and also exhausting eight days. I was working one-on-one with these wonderful people. They would be lined up as soon as we pulled up to the church in the morning. Some would be there all day, waiting for their turn. I never heard a complaint or a grumble about having to wait up to six hours in the hot sun. They were so grateful to have the blessing of being chosen to be there. It might be the only time they would have the opportunity.

I say it was exhausting because, working so closely with them, I saw the poverty, the need, and the never-ending line. By day three, my friend Arlene suggested strongly that I spend a day on the construction site. I was getting so down and dispirited about how little these people had. Again, that need to fix everything. Yet they were so happy with what we were able to do for them. My most memorable experience was with a little old lady. I'm sure she was in her eighties. She had waited all day, almost to the end, to be seen. When I outfitted her with a pair that would suit her, she beamed. Through her interpreter, she told me how she would now be able to read her Bible! Well, I was sobbing again.

We managed to see 650 people during our eyeglass clinic, and we fit 450 with glasses. A couple of teenage girls came through who had perfect vision but insisted they couldn't really see well at school. After examining them thoroughly and finding nothing wrong, I called Michelle over. She walked over to the glasses table, selected a pair, and had the girl try them on. She then went through the chart and the girl was able to see perfectly. The girl left with her glasses in hand and a huge smile on her face. I asked Michelle if I had missed anything in the exam, as the girl didn't seem to need glasses. Michelle assured me that all was well; she had given the girl a pair of clear glass. The girl had no vision problem … she just wanted a pair of glasses. Michelle had seen this before, so she carried glasses with clear lenses. The girl could save face and still have something to show. No harm done! When you have so little, this was a lot.

When I see my students board the bus sporting new glasses, I always make a point of telling them how good they look wearing them. Some know of my experience with the eyeglass clinic in Bluefields and are just amazed at the primitive ways of examining.

So, if you come across an old pair of glasses in your junk drawer and don't know what to do with them, take them to your local eye clinic and drop them off. Somewhere in the world, somebody will benefit from them. I would love to work at another eyeglass clinic if the opportunity presents itself. I'd be there in the blink of an eye!

CHAPTER FIFTEEN

BACK HOME

I returned to work after my trip to Bluefields with a different attitude and gratitude for all I had. I was on a high for a couple of weeks after I returned, but I eventually returned to earth and back to the routine of work, paying bills, cleaning house, and generally complaining about all of the above. I enjoyed my job as a baker in the long-term care centre, but the physical aspect was starting to wear on me. This was an industrial kitchen, with industrial-sized equipment. The wear and tear of lugging heavy bins and pans and making huge batches of everything for 150 people, by myself, was getting hard on the body. I was going to the chiropractor once a week and applying cold packs and heating pads to my neck and shoulders when I got home. I made the decision that as much as I enjoyed the job, I couldn't continue battering myself. I gave my notice and bid goodbye to my friends I had started with.

From there I went to a local grocery store and worked in the deli department for a few months. It was a job. I just couldn't see me retiring from it. I felt like I was putting in time but with no real direction. I didn't have real ties to the job, and it certainly wasn't going to be a long-lasting career. But I had to work. I couldn't just stay home; I would go crazy within a couple of weeks. My husband made a good living, and he was very supportive of whatever I decided to do. I just didn't know what I wanted to do!

This was about May/June 2013.

I was having coffee with Arlene one afternoon, complaining about my woes and lack of oomph for my job. I started asking her about bus driving. She'd been driving for close to fifteen years by this time. It was just an offhand remark. She told me how she loved her job, how she had plenty of time in between her bus runs to do other things, and she actually worked three jobs. She had full benefits with the bus company, excellent training, and a freedom she'd never had in other jobs. My interest was piqued. Before I could think too much about it, I went to the site online and applied for a bus driver position.

At that time, the Foothills bus division was looking to train and hire a few drivers. There was no guarantee of a permanent route, but you could at least get a foot in the door. The training was all free, in-class as well as on the road. Within a few days of applying, I received a call from the office asking me to come in for an interview. I met with Virginia, who was the superintendent of the buses and drivers. We chatted for a while, and she told me she'd get back to me. Meanwhile, I had started the paperwork required for the position. I went to the local R.C.M.P. detachment and got an updated driver abstract and a police check, and then I filled in an application in High River at the town office to give permission for a child check investigation. This is to ensure that there are no red flags in my working with children. This last one would take about six weeks to get back.

I received a call from Virginia a few days after my interview, letting me know I was to start my training! They were awesome to work around my schedule. I was still working at the deli, so a few days a week I went in for training. About seven of us took the training together. We took part in the classroom training, going over all the rules and regulations and safety dos and don'ts. It was very thorough and intensive training. We then made our way out to the actual bus. Have you ever seen one of these up close? They're HUGE; they're MONSTROUS. Being in class and being on the bus were two different things. How was I ever going to drive this thing? For the first time since I'd applied for this career change, I was having second thoughts. Who did I think I was? I couldn't do this. Fortunately, my three wonderful trainers—Lise-Anne, Penny, and Shannon—were used to this. My fellow classmates were also experiencing this apprehension, this eye-popping fear. Arlene was in touch with me throughout my training, cheering and encouraging me on.

Our training was very thorough, very in-depth. We're dealing with a huge responsibility here. I was so nervous and frightened that I would forget something, that I would mess up and be responsible for a catastrophe. This was all before I even sat in the driver's seat! Years ago, I took a driving course through AMA in Calgary. I was twenty-five years old the first time I got behind the wheel of a vehicle. Driving was not a top priority for me. The bus system in the city was good enough to get me around. I asked the man I was with at that time if he could drive me somewhere, and he said no, he didn't want to. The next day, I phoned AMA and booked a driving course that would start within a week. I had my 1977 Ford Pinto station wagon parked in my driveway before the course was finished. I was not going to be at anybody's mercy ever again for a ride.

I went for my driver's license and failed the first time. A bit more practise and I passed. I was on my way. Watch out, Calgary! I'm very glad I learned to drive in the city. Like anything else, repetition and practice go a long way. You don't drive Deerfoot Trail, you survive it! This thoroughfare connects Calgary from the four corners of the city. It's a fast-paced, at times congested highway. A smaller scale version of the Highway 401 that runs through parts of Ontario. I've been very blessed and fortunate that I've never been in an accident in all my years of driving. I'm a cautious and defensive driver.

The training I went through with the bus division was top-notch. Every aspect and scenario we could think of was covered. We learned every corner of that bus—under the hood, all the fluids, what to check for, what to look for in every tire and every inch of this beast. Then and only then were we allowed to sit behind the wheel. Wow! What a view! Then we had to learn all of the goings-on inside the bus, including all the safety and emergency exits and windows, what this button does, mirrors, mirrors, mirrors.

We have to check all our lights, hazards, ambers, flashing reds, and stop sign. Is all our paperwork on the bus in order? Insurance, registration, provincial tickets, CVIC certificates? Is our fire extinguisher up to date? Do we have our triangles for the roadway stowed away? How about our First Aid kit? Is it fully stocked, along with our biohazard kit? This last one is necessary if a student throws up on the bus. This kit contains an absorbent to use, kind of like kitty litter. Thankfully, I've never had to use it!

Every bus is different as to where everything is, even the lights and the parking brake. They all run differently and behave differently, just like a child. It's good to have your own bus appointed to you for that specific route, so that you can get to know all its creaks and groans, how it turns, where the turning radius is, and what to expect from it in bad weather. It's like your own personal vehicle. You get to know how it handles. I had my bus for four years, and I loved it. It was a great 2009 Thomas C2, seventy-two-passenger bus.

It was taken away to use as a spare bus, as we were low on "good" spare buses. If your bus is in for a semi-annual service, or if you need something repaired, you have to get a spare bus. UGHHHH! I hate spare buses! You have to learn everything all over again, and depending how long you have it and the time of year, it can be very annoying. Yeah! I'm spoiled! I like my bus. I know my bus. I was upgraded to a 2016 Blue Bird when they took my bus. Most people jump at the chance to get a newer bus. Not me. I eventually got used to it and made it my own. It wasn't comfortable like my C2. It had no storage room at all, although it did have features that my old one didn't. It had power mirrors! Wow, the envy from other drivers who didn't have this feature was palpable. This was a big deal. Do you know what's it like to climb up and try to adjust your side mirrors, climb back down and check, and then climb back up to repeat the whole process? If my mirrors aren't positioned just right, it can be a hazard. I have to be able to see everything around me. You might think that because I have thirty-odd windows on the bus, I should have no problem, but there are so many blind spots on buses. The newer bus I got had a split windshield. This in itself was irritating after having had a full screen for four years. There's a black band right down the middle of the windshield to separate the two sides. This acts as a blind spot. When you come up to a country stop sign, the door itself acts as a blind spot, hiding the oncoming traffic to my right. Hence, I always wait an extra three to four seconds to make sure nobody is in that blind spot. This has been a saving grace a few times.

When I had to change buses, my students were very vocal and annoyed about the change. They loved our old bus! They knew it as well as I did. But we adapted. We made the new bus our own. I decorated it with magnets and butterfly stickers, and I'd decorate it for different occasions. Two years into having this new bus, I happened to be at the right place at the right time, and someone mentioned that my old bus might be available to take back. I jumped at the chance. It was still in great shape, and, yes, I could take it. I cleaned her up from top to bottom and transferred all my stuff over to it. I didn't tell my students till I pulled up to the school with it one afternoon. Those who had been on this one before were hollering! They were ecstatic to have it back. Seriously! It's just a bus, right? It was our bus. I've come to realize that my young students like to have something of their own. In life, it's usually parents, teachers, and other adults who make decisions. My students took pride in our bus; they knew that 22 was their domain. As typical of human nature, they don't like change. It's nice to know that some things will remain the same. It's a sense of security to know that when the bus comes around the corner, it's going to be their bus. Don't be messing with it. They have little control in the say of their everyday goings-on, so being able to point to their bus and say "That's mine" is a good thing. It doesn't take much to make them happy and secure.

CHAPTER SIXTEEN

COVID-19

I was into my seventh year driving my route with the same students, a few new ones, and a few that had graduated to high school. We had gone through the fall and into Christmas; we celebrated Groundhog Day followed by Valentine's Day. We'd survived another Alberta winter and were all looking forward to spring. Windows were cracked open on sunny days, layers were being shed, and the sight of returning geese was a welcomed gift.

There had been grumblings and rumours going around about a super virus that was affecting people globally. I really wasn't too concerned about this, as I foolishly thought that we in Okotoks, Alberta were safely removed from any and all germs pertaining to what was to be called coronavirus and then renamed Covid-19. Silly me! The world as we knew it would be forever altered, turned upside down and inside out. This was the stuff of sci-fi movies; this was too surreal. This wasn't just a rumour anymore. This was happening. The nightly news was all about the case counts all over the world and in our own country, province, and town. The incessant buzzing about this virus was breaking out all over. We were on a need-to-know basis. Talk about feeling powerless! We waited with bated breath to hear from Prime Minister Trudeau and Premier Jason Kenney as to the next steps. It still didn't feel like this deserved the attention it was getting. Ignorance is a bliss.

March 12, 2020 was a Thursday. I dropped my students off after school. Seeing as we had the next day off as a PD day, the students were allowed to sit where they wanted, using this as a Free Friday day. As I said goodbye to them, I wished them all a good weekend and told them I'd see them on Monday morning. We would not see each other again till September.

We received the call from the superintendent of schools that evening. We were told that we'd be shut down for two weeks due to the virus. In the interim, we were to go and clean our buses as well as sanitize them from top to bottom. Every square inch was to be scoured and scrubbed. We fully expected to be back in operation by the end of March. I was in contact with the parents and relayed whatever information I had.

The next call came, and again we were told to hold still. We would be off till after Easter. By now it was starting to sink in that this might be serious. The news was all about it. You could no longer ignore it. It was right in our back yard. Easter came and went, and we were told that we weren't going back till September. By this time, online learning was being set up. Bus drivers received our layoff slips, and we were able to apply for CERB, the Canada Emergency Response Benefit, which was a financial support for employed and self-employed Canadians who were directly affected by Covid-19 These were uncertain times, to say the least. I hadn't even been able to say goodbye to my students. Nobody knew this would happen, and we weren't prepared.

It was such a sad and confusing time. I didn't want to watch the news anymore; I was shell-shocked from the tragedies around the world. I wasn't concerned about contracting this virus. If I were to get infected, I knew that God was in charge. Certainly my life changed. I only went to the stores for necessities, and I tried to be mindful and respectful of other people. I felt the anger and angst radiating from people as I went shopping for groceries. The paranoia and outright fear from these people I had once considered friendly and warm was overwhelming. We were living in a perpetual deer-in-the-headlight look.

I don't do well with too much time on my hands. Usually, the two months we have off in the summer is plenty. Now I would be looking at five months. What was I going to do? I missed the students, the routine of my job, my purpose. Prior to this, I was active in volunteering in town with the Mission Thrift Store as well as the local food bank. I also enjoyed delivering Meals on Wheels. I decided that if I couldn't work, I wanted to help the community where I could. I upped my volunteering at the thrift store to three days a week and took on more shifts with Meals on Wheels. I continued with the food bank. I needed to do this to keep myself busy, to give back to the community that was slowly falling apart. Doing this was a blessing for me and kept me grounded. I didn't want to fall into the abyss of loneliness and depression that was all too common during this time. I am so grateful that I had this lifeline to grasp.

Most volunteers at the thrift store as well as the food bank are elderly. During the peak months of the virus, many of our elders opted to stay home for fear of contracting the Covid. The thrift store did close down for a month, with quite a few volunteers not returning when it reopened. The food bank is an essential service for our community, so we didn't close down, although we did alter how we served our clients. Hampers were brought to the vehicles, clients weren't allowed in the building, and strict cleaning policies were enforced. We couldn't afford to be shut down. The client intake was rising, as jobs were lost, income was down, and people were needing assistance now more than ever.

Meals on Wheels was also a very important aid to our community, now more than ever. We couldn't stop bringing meals to our clients. We adjusted to different ways of picking up the food, gloved up, and masked up. Our top priority was the safety of our vulnerable clients. We did it, we worked together, and we persevered.

I believe the first six months of Covid-19 marked how strong the human spirit is. I also believe God was and is and will be with us throughout it all. A person's true character shines through during these times. All of us experienced a varied list of emotions: anger, fear, confusion, hatred, shame, paranoia, depression, loneliness, rage. But along with these, we also must not forget what else came from this: a sense of pride as we helped our neighbours, a closeness we felt to our community, a coming together to see what could be done. Everyday heroes stood up to the plate. Teachers and parents worked together to get online schooling up and running. Families spent more time together out of necessity, but I believe a lot of good came from that. We were getting back to basics: meals around the kitchen table, yard work during the summer, and projects that had been put off.

I have this image of God in heaven listening to us humans as we complain about how little time there is in a day, and that we can't get everything done that needs doing. If only we had more time! Well, guess what—we got more time. That deck you've been putting off got built. The purge of your house was completed, and boxes of donations were brought to the thrift store. We received so many donations, there were days we actually had to refuse them. It seems everybody in town was cleaning out their houses. It was incredible the amount of stuff that came in. This in turn goes on our shelves and gets sold, and the money goes back into the community. This money went to help a women's shelter, the food bank, and many more organizations. Out of disaster a blessing arose. Even with the month that the thrift store was closed, sales for the year were outstanding. The most popular items were puzzles and game boards. We couldn't keep them in the store. Families were staying home, they were connecting and playing together. Books flew off the shelf, as did crafts. If you have to stay home, you can't travel, and it's just you and your immediate family, you have to make the best of it. I was reminded of growing up in Ontario. We had a cottage with no phone and very basic cable. We would sit around at night playing cards and building puzzles. We read a lot, and we had fun.

It's interesting that we were given this time, albeit it's probably not the way we anticipated having spare time, but we had it. How did you spend your time?

I felt like there was unfinished business with my students. As I said, I wasn't even able to say goodbye to them. It was all so abrupt. We had no warning, no lead up to the finale. I always passed out treats on our last day and wished each and every one of them, big and little, a wonderful summer. Some of the older students who would be going on to high school in the fall, I wouldn't see again. This was it. I don't know if it actually dawned on them, but it was a big deal for me. Some of these kids had been on my bus for the full seven years I'd been driving, and now they were gone.

At the end of June, I phoned my boss lady, Wanda, and asked if it were possible to get the address of my students. I had their phone numbers but not their addresses. I wanted to drop off cards to say hello and to wish them a wonderful summer, assuring them that I'd be back in the fall on their bus. Because of FOIP (Freedom of Information and Protection of Privacy Act), I wasn't allowed access to their mailing addresses. Totally understandable. So, I did the next best thing. I phoned all my parents and explained that I'd like to send a card to the kids, but because of privacy I didn't have their addresses. If they felt comfortable giving it to me, that was great; if they didn't, I totally understood. Every single parent I phoned was more then willing to help out. For the next week, I penned, addressed, and sealed individual cards to all my students. If there were siblings, they each got one. After all, they are individuals, not just a unit. I had a blast coming up with personal greetings to all my kids. Now it felt finished. I was able to say goodbye to them. I received many emails from parents saying how well the cards had gone over. The kids were thrilled to get a card in the mailbox. So cool!

Throughout the summer months, a few of my parents kept in touch with me, asking how my summer was going, letting me know how the kids were doing, and asking if I was coming back in the fall. They were very anxious, as were the kids, to return to school! I actually phoned Wanda at the shop and asked if I could take the bus around my route and honk the horn and wave to my kids and see how many parents came running out. She said no.

The third week of August, we were told to come in and make sure our buses were totally cleaned and sanitized. We would then pick up our paperwork for the new year of schooling. This entailed our student list, parents contact numbers, and any changes to the route. This is always a hectic time; we have about a week to contact all parents and give them information on pick-up times and drop-off. We also have to draw maps of our route, finalize seating arrangements, and prepare what we call a fan out list, which is needed in case of emergency where the bus is not running. I assign six of my parents the phone numbers of six or seven other parents, and the call goes out within minutes that the bus won't be running. It's a wonderful way to get the news out there quickly. I basically call one parent, and she calls the other six, who then call the remainder. When you have fifty to sixty students, this is the quickest and most efficient way to get the word out. Every year when I enlist my parents for this, they have always been so helpful and forthcoming.

As with everything, this year would be different because of Covid-19. As a rule, I allow the students to sit with whoever they wish, providing there is no horsing around or fighting. Once it's established where every student is going to sit, I then make a seating plan, which is turned into the office and a copy kept on my bus. This is necessary in case of emergency; there has to be a record of what student was seated in which seat. Their name tags are then placed by their seats. Now, things would be different. Friends could no longer sit together. Students had to sit by themselves, unless they had siblings on the bus, and then they would have to sit with them. This did not go over well with some siblings! I actually had to separate two brothers and sit them by themselves because they spent the whole bus ride beating on each other. I had some siblings with one in grade nine and the other in grade one sitting together. As another addition to this bizzarro bus ride, the students from grades four to twelve were mandated to wear masks. Kindergarten to grade three was optional. We carried a box of masks on the bus, because you know someone is going to forget theirs. I had no issues with the students wearing masks. They were all very cooperative. They were all learning to adapt to the new normal that was their lives now. Young people are so much more flexible than their older counterparts. They look to us for guidance, and they follow our example. Please, God, let me be a good example.

CHAPTER SEVENTEEN

BACK ON THE BUS...YEAR 8

September 2, 2020

The alarm went off at 5:00 a.m. I hadn't slept much, as I was too excited. Like a kid at Christmas, I jumped out of bed, anticipating this day at long last. I showered, ate, prayed for a good, safe day, and headed out to the bus depot. The bus has been cleaned and was ready to go. I did my pre-trip, making sure everything was good to go. I had placed all the name tags up so the students would know where to sit as they came in. The first students would be going right to the back, and the second pick-up would sit up front. This way there would be no crossing each other. That was the idea, anyway. At that time, everything was by trial and error. Some people might think we were a little overboard, or that we were being too stringent, but better to err on the side of caution than to reap the aftermath of not being cautious.

I approached my first pick-up stop, honking the horn and waving like a crazy woman. Close to twenty students were waiting in a line, all of them wearing masks. So many of them had grown over the five months since I'd seen them last. They boarded the bus, and I directed them right to the back and told them to find their seats.

SUBDUED is the word that came to mind. They were so quiet, looking so out of place. We picked up the second crew, and they were just as quiet. I was spooked by that point. Where were my day-one-of-school students? Where was the noise and laughter and banter? I had to keep checking my rear-view mirror to make sure they were actually on the bus. I tried to make small talk as I was driving, but with a mask on it was hard for them to hear.

We got to the school, where usually we would sit until 8:25 a.m. before letting loose ten busloads of students (roughly four hundred students). Because of Covid, we dropped them off as we came in. This would cut down on too many kids crossing each other's paths. I certainly didn't envy the teachers. There were so many rules and regulations in place now; every T had to be crossed and every I dotted. The poor students were in a state of shock, and rightly so. They didn't know what they were allowed to touch or not touch, and they were sequestered in one room all day so as not to come in contact with other classes. The teachers rotated to different classes. Lunch was eaten in classes, and recess was split up at different times for different classes.

As bus drivers, we were responsible for disinfecting the bus twice a day, making sure all surfaces touched by hands were thoroughly cleaned. We couldn't take a chance of contamination. We were told that if a child was on the bus with symptoms of coughing and sneezing, we would have to let the office know, and keep the child on the bus till someone from the school came and collected them. The parent would then have to come and get them. Keep in mind that this was the beginning of the school year when germs run amok. This is the norm. But due to Covid, what once was just a regular run of the mill cold now got you quarantined at home for fourteen days.

The student would be sent home and sent to get tested. When the test came back negative, they could return. I didn't have any positive cases reported on my bus. I did have students out for the fourteen-day isolation period because someone in their class tested positive, so the whole class was sent home for the duration. My grade eight students were all off the bus for two weeks.

This whole experience was a learning curve for everybody: parents, teachers, bus drivers, and students. Over the next few weeks and months, we all settled into some semblance of a routine. The students were relaxing a little more. The bus was sounding a little more boisterous. Halloween came and went. I decorated the bus as usual, but we couldn't give out treats for fear of contamination. I know it's not a big deal, but it just felt like it was another thing that was being taken away from the kids. We were so fortunate in so many ways. Our kids were going to school; they were getting an education, and they were going to be OK. It's not the end of the world to have to give something up for the security and safety of a healthy future. As we go, we grow. We are seeing what works and what doesn't. We are learning to bend and adapt. We will come out of this through the grace of God. I totally believe this.

We celebrated Christmas and the New Year with enthusiasm, looking forward to better days. There were a few hiccups along the way, cases exploding at the high school, shutdowns again, businesses opening only to close again. We have the vaccine now, which will make its way to all Canadians. We are so fortunate to be in a country where we have access to this if we choose to. We have the freedom that so many across the globe are denied.

At I write this, it is March 8, 2021. Yes, there is still a road ahead of us to travel, but we are getting there. There is hope. I will continue driving the bus, and God willing, I will wish my students an awesome summer. I learned a long time ago that you can make a plan, but don't plan the outcome. Anything can happen. Covid-19 is a great example of that. My goal is to drive for another four years. By then, I will have seen the kindergarten kids that first came on my bus graduate from high school. That will be a full cycle of education. I think that's a good note to end on.

And now, a final thought.

Throughout the eight years that I have been at the helm of route 22, I have accomplished a few things.

I have driven a total of 224,000 kilometres picking up students.

I have certified for First Aid three times.

I have certified for Fire and Safety twice.

I have renewed my Class 2 driver's license four times.

I returned to Nicaragua two more times.

I zip-lined in Managua, Nicaragua.

I called in sick twice.

I laid my mother to rest.

I had my gallbladder removed. (hence calling in sick)

I have welcomed five great-grandchildren (all boys) into this world.

I buried my dog and cat (old age).

I adopted two kittens from Pound Rescue. (What was I thinking?)

I went to court nine times for people not stopping for the bus lights.

I have had cameras installed on the outside of my bus, in order to monitor drivers going through my lights. To date, I have recorded 2 offenders within a 2- week period.

I was baptized.

I flew to Ontario to surprise my sister Debbie on her sixtieth birthday.

I have never been in an accident. (Thank you, God.)

I have had a few close calls and one very, very nasty almost got T-boned, hair-raising scare.

I have laughed at the antics of my students.

I have celebrated my sixtieth birthday.

I have written a book.

I hope you have enjoyed my musings and memoirs. I have certainly enjoyed putting it to paper. When you see the yellow school bus coming down the road, give a wave to the driver. Please remember, we have your precious cargo on our buses. We will return them; we're not allowed to keep them

God bless you all. He certainly has blessed me.

If I could ask for one bus wish, it would be that my students speak fondly of me as their bus driver. If asked what their experience as a bus kid was, may they say it was awesome.

I read the description of a bus driver as being:

Someone who watches 40 to 60 screaming kids in a mirror while driving a 40ft box on wheels. What do you do?

ACKNOWLEDGEMENTS

"And whatever you do, whether in word or deed, do it all in the name of the Lord Jesus, giving thanks to God and the Father through him" (Colossians 3:17).

I owe a bus load of gratitude to my computer angels who helped me navigate through the scary and confusing jargon of computer speak, especially, my sister Debbie, I love you so much for not hanging up on me when I would call and yell HELP! I could sense the frustration coming through the phone lines from three thousand kilometres away, and the many prayers. I will think about taking a computer course. And to Kim L., who came over one afternoon and compiled everything for me, and made sure I hit SAVE. thank you, and to Debbie H. from our bus office who tried her best to help me when I didn't even know what it wa, I was trying to accomplish.

Thank you to my sister in Christ, Cindy, who encouraged me to share my story.

To my dear friend Arlene Howard: Thank you for your quiet, encouraging example of living life with Jesus. I will always treasure our time in Nicaragua, and our friendship. As well as the many phone calls to you when I first started driving the bus, and you would tell me to" just breathe."

To Tellwell Publishing: Thank you for making this so easy for me. Every aspect of this journey has been dealt with in grace and patience. Jun Vertudazo, my project manager, you showed great professional candor with my lack of computer skills, and you were always available to me. To my editor Kerry, thank you for showing me a different approach to my writing. You were very kind and gentle.

To Foothills School Division: Thank you for being such a wonderful, caring, and fun place to work. I look forward to putting on many more miles.

To all my incredible, awesome students on route 22 out of Heritage Heights School: You all are the reason for this book.

To all my fellow bus drivers, and to all bus drivers everywhere: Thank you for what you do.

To my one and only child, Misty, I love you baby.

Last, but certainly not least, to my husband, Jim: Thank you for your support on this. You've never said no to me. You are the pen to my paper.

bmerkley19@gmail.com